# Unmasking

Interview with

# Dr. Wolfgang Smith

Triumph Communications
www.triumphcommunications.net

# Note

*Unmasking the Faces of Antichrist* is a written interview between mathematician, retired university professor, and author Dr. Wolfgang Smith and Canadian journalist and publisher Bernard Janzen. Dr. Smith is the author of:

*Cosmos and Transcendence: Breaking Through the Barrier of Scientistic Belief*

*Theistic Evolution: The Teilhardian Heresy*

*The Quantum Enigma: Finding the Hidden Key*

*Ancient Wisdom and Modern Misconceptions: A Critique of Contemporary Scientism*

*Science and Myth: With a Response to Stephen Hawking's The Grand Design*

*In Quest of Catholicity: Malachi Martin Responds to Wolfgang Smith*

The book *In Quest of Catholicity* is a compilation of an exchange of letters between Dr. Smith and former Vatican insider, exorcist, and best-selling author Malachi Martin. This book is available from Triumph Communications. Still available from Triumph Communications are eight books in interview format with Malachi Martin: *Catholicism Overturned*, *The Eternal War*, *The Kingdom of Darkness*, *Shoes of the Fisherman*, *Peter in Chains*, *The Deserted Vineyard*, *The Tempter's Hour*, and *Crossing the Desert*.

© 2017 Triumph Communications
ISBN 978-1-928102-17-5
Printed and published in Canada by Triumph Communications.
Website: www.triumphcommunications.net

*To my beloved wife,*

*Thea Smith*

Eternal rest grant unto her soul, O Lord;

And let perpetual light shine upon her.

May she rest in peace.

Amen.

# Table of Contents

# Preface

Readers of *Unmasking the Faces of Antichrist* may be intrigued by the title of the book. While we are not yet living under the direct rule of the Antichrist, the world we live in is being increasingly shaped by the actions of the precursors of the Antichrist. Today there are various fields of activity by Antichrist forces which in the end times will eventually coalesce into a single visible force. These fields of activity are still heavily camouflaged, as the precursors to the Antichrist are not yet open regarding the true nature of their agenda. The architects of the New World Order and their multiple designs are masked. In this book, Dr. Wolfgang Smith unmasks these designs which are rapidly reshaping modern civilization.

Part I of this book, *Malachi Martin: Servant of Christ*, explains the vital role that Malachi Martin played and continues to play in assisting souls who are struggling with the deepest crisis in the Catholic Church's history. Among the scholars of the post-conciliar period, what Fr. Martin uniquely provides is an explanation of the crisis in its entirety, including its supernatural origins.

In Part II, *Science, Scientism, and Christological Cosmology*, Dr. Smith deals with the extremely important subject of science. As a scientist, he is aware of the critical role science plays in shaping mankind's view of the cosmos, which in turn affects mankind's religious beliefs. Modern scientists have presented a worldview that has made the traditional Christian view of the cosmos appear obscurantist, leading to the diminishing of religious belief. Dr. Smith shows that this anti-Christian view of the cosmos, far from being based on scientific findings, is in fact ideology-driven from start to finish. Employing the term "scientism" to refer to these spurious cosmological tenets, he identifies that movement as one of the contemporary "faces of Antichrist" warring against Christianity.

Part III, *How to Survive as a Catholic in an Anti-Catholic World*, is a chapter of extreme relevancy. Dr. Smith confronts a critical dilemma facing Catholic families, that of university education. On one hand, as a former university professor, he explains how modern university education has often become one of the faces of Antichrist. On the other hand, there is a need for good Catholic doctors, lawyers, scientists, etc. In this chapter, Dr. Smith provides guidance on how to deal with this dilemma, which indeed is representative of contemporary civilization at large, and as such concerns us all.

Dr. Smith concludes by showing that we must choose between Christ and Antichrist. There is no neutrality in this cosmic battle. In *Unmasking the Faces of Antichrist*, Dr. Wolfgang Smith makes a unique and necessary contribution to maintaining the faith of our fathers and shines a light on the path that we must take to reach our eternal destiny.

# Part I
# Malachi Martin: Servant of Christ

**Dr. Wolfgang Smith, could you please tell us a bit about yourself and your background. What is your profession?**

It was during my high school years that I first became interested in fundamental questions touching upon science, philosophy and theology. I cannot tell what exactly prompted that interest, that inner drive; I only know that it had little to do with any outer influence. Meanwhile I could hardly wait to enter a university, in the belief that this is where clarity in "high" matters is finally to be attained. But by the time I graduated from Cornell at age eighteen—with majors in physics, mathematics, and philosophy—I had become profoundly disenchanted in that regard. Let me be clear: whereas both physics and mathematics fascinated me greatly—as they do to this day—I realized, soon enough, that access to "the high things" pertains *de jure* to the province of philosophy, or more precisely: to the twin disciplines of philosophy and theology. And there was the rub: for it likewise became clear to me that, as a present-day academic discipline—humanized and secularized to the hilt!—philosophy is dead. This left me with physics and mathematics as a prospective career.

After taking an M.S. in physics from Purdue University I spent three years at Bell Aircraft Corporation in the capacity of an aerodynamicist, following which I took a Ph.D. in mathematics from Columbia and embarked finally upon a professorial career in that field. I subsequently taught at several universities, including M.I.T. and UCLA. Unbeknownst, however, to my colleagues, I continued to pursue serious studies in the domain of philosophy, and eventually began to write, first a series of articles for the *Homiletic & Pastoral Review*, and in time a sequence of books. My intent was, first, to apprise a largely unsuspecting public of the fact that, in the name of science, they had been duped into accepting a modern-day myth, a kind of pseudo-religion one could almost say—and subsequent to this essential clarification, to re-affirm, in terms comprehensible to contemporary readers, some of the principal verities of authentic philosophy.

**How did you get to know Malachi Martin? Had you read his books before you met him?**

I first met Malachi Martin on April 28, 1997. By then I was retired, and my wife and I were living in northern Idaho. I was sitting at my desk that morning when the telephone rang: someone representing a radio talk program wanted to know whether I would join Malachi Martin about an hour hence in a discussion relating to "science and religion"; and so, not long thereafter, we met "on the air." Having evidently read my first book, Fr. Martin sent a few related questions my way to bring out certain pertinent points, to which he responded magnanimously, and with his usual eloquence; and thus began an exchange of ideas which was to continue till the end of his life. Apart from a rather intensive correspondence—which has since been published—we also made ample use of the telephone; but alas, we had only one face-to-face meeting, in November of 1998. As you can well understand, I treasure the memory of those few precious and irreplaceable days.

I had not read any of Malachi Martin's books prior to our first meeting, and must confess that to this day I have read only a handful. Of course, I did subsequently read what is perhaps his *magnum opus*, *Windswept House*, which impressed me greatly. What I knew about Malachi Martin from the start is that he championed doctrinal orthodoxy and the Tridentine Mass; and this in itself aroused my admiration and high esteem.

**When you met Fr. Martin, what were your first impressions?**

An apt question: for it happens that my first impressions of Fr. Martin are indeed memorable. What struck me almost from the moment he opened the door and welcomed me into his presence is not easy to describe; the single word that comes closest is perhaps "kindness." Not an ordinary kindness—not a mere friendliness—but a benignity that instantly sweeps away barriers: a *spiritual* kindness, I am tempted to say. The fact is that Malachi Martin was all priest, and thus, in very truth, a *spiritual father* to everyone who came into his presence with even a modicum of receptivity. We will never know how many lives he touched, nor how many souls he saved. I recall in this connection a small incident at the Park

Plaza, which has stuck in my memory all these years: it happened when a hat check girl handed Fr. Martin his overcoat as we left the restaurant. I remember to this day how he turned to her and spoke a few words: ordinary words, which I have long since forgotten. Yet I sensed that something had been transmitted which perhaps will remain with that person for the rest of her life. Let me repeat: Malachi Martin was all priest—all Jesuit in fact—perpetually and forever in the service of the Roman Catholic Church.

**What did you learn of his work from your conversations with Malachi Martin?**

Let me say, first of all, that I did not interrogate Malachi Martin in this regard. What particularly concerned me at the time were broad issues relating to the Church and the modern world. We did however have wide-ranging conversations, in the course of which Fr. Martin told us a good deal about his own involvement with what he termed "the underground church," which as you will recall, he described in one of your interviews as "an underground network of Masses, baptisms, confessions, bishops, priests, nuns, seminaries, and libraries…" He left no doubt that he himself not only participated actively in that "church" as a priest, but supported the movement in any way possible. We had the distinct impression that he was in close touch with many of the priests involved in this enterprise, that he offered advice and guidance, and spared no effort in promoting that cause in the conviction that "the real Church is going underground." At one point, Malachi Martin mentioned, in passing, that he was at the time carrying a large number of "underground" priests on his payroll: former diocesan priests, namely, who had been expelled by their bishops for their refusal to discard the traditions of our faith, especially the Tridentine rite of Mass.

**Did Malachi Martin believe that the underground Church was necessary? Fr. Martin believed that the life of the institutional Church will mirror the life of Christ and in these times is on the road to Calvary. The institutional Church appears to be liquidating itself and is headed for entombment. Is Pope Francis hastening this process by destroying the credibility of**

**the institutional Church, especially the Papacy?**

Malachi Martin did, most assuredly, perceive the underground Church to be necessary, in keeping with his conviction that the Tridentine—or what he preferred to call the Roman—rite of Mass constitutes the liturgical heart and center of the Catholic Church. He therefore perceived its abolition as an inherently nefarious act: an expression in fact of "Lucifer's own hatred for Calvary, because the Mass *is* Calvary" to put it in his own words. Now, given the fact that the post-Conciliar Church is indeed bent upon this abolition—that is to say, the permanent replacement of the Roman rite by the Novus Ordo—one can readily understand why Malachi Martin was adamant regarding the necessity of an underground Church. First and foremost, it is needed for the preservation of the authentic sacramental order of the Roman Catholic Church, beginning with the Mass that "*is* Calvary."

The fact that the institutional Church is presently re-enacting the Passion of Jesus on the road to Calvary is becoming more apparent almost with every passing month. What particularly strikes me in that regard—besides the betrayal of Christ by churchmen of the highest ranks—is the horrific spectacle of humiliation and disfigurement. I fully concur, moreover, that "the institutional Church appears to be liquidating itself," a process which began visibly with Paul VI, was continued under John Paul II, and is quite obviously attaining unprecedented levels of destructive ferocity under the present pontificate.

There can be no doubt that Pope Francis is indeed "destroying the credibility" of the Church over which he presides. He does so not only by subjecting to scorn and ridicule those who still uphold the time-honored practices of the pre-Conciliar Catholic Church, but by contradicting some of its basic doctrines, such as the indissolubility of marriage and the sinfulness of adultery. It is clear that he has his mind set on radically restructuring the institutional Church in points of doctrine, discipline, and overall orientation in keeping with his far-out leftist ideology.

You raised the question whether Pope Francis is hastening the ongoing liquidation of the institutional Church by destroying its credibility; and I ask myself: what more could he do in that regard? We are presently witnessing a veritable *reductio ad absurdum* of the post-Conciliar Church, the likes of which could scarcely have been imagined before the present Bishop of Rome appeared upon the scene. It seems to me that once a pope promulgates doctrines that plainly contradict fundamental dogmas of the Church, the destruction to which you allude has in essence been consummated. Of course, one can always invent additional heresies and undertake further steps in the ongoing campaign of unconditional *aggiornamento*: my point is that, even so, the walls have already been breached, the die already cast.

Actually, we know from Malachi Martin's revelations that the walls were breached long before the arrival of Pope Francis; as Fr. Martin informs us in the Prologue to *Windswept House*: "The Enthronement of the Fallen Archangel Lucifer was effected within the Roman Catholic Citadel on June 29, 1963," eight days after the election of Pope Paul VI. That enthronement, as we are further told, was effected by the celebration of a Black Mass in the Chapel of St. Paul within the precincts of the Vatican. At that moment, the die was cast: what Malachi Martin calls "a superforce" was thus unleashed within the institutional Church, henceforth to impede the pope from exercising the Petrine power of the keys. From that day forward the reigning popes have been manifestly unable to unmask the Enemy in their midst, powerless to thwart his subversive influence. What Pope Francis adds to the scene is that he seems fully and joyfully to embrace the new directives lock, stock, and barrel, with an enthusiasm which in fact has not been seen since the heady days of the Council. Where John Paul II had qualms— for example, when it comes to the institution of marriage—Francis quite obviously has none, and where his German predecessor labored to reconcile the old and the new by way of what he termed a "hermeneutic of continuity," it is plainly evident that the Argentinian leftist could hardly care less. An unmasking, clearly, of the vaunted "spirit of Vatican II" is presently in progress before the eyes of an astonished world: what happened in the darkness of night on June 29, 1963, is now coming to light.

**There is a period in Fr. Martin's life that is largely unknown, which is his work behind the Iron Curtain during the Cold War. You were very privileged to have discussed that experience with him, as he generally did not mention this experience in public interviews. What do you know of his experiences behind the Iron Curtain? Do you think this experience played an important role in the development of his analysis of the crisis of modern civilization and of the Church?**

There is one bit of information I learned in conversation which does shed light upon that hidden period in his life. My wife and I were having a pleasant talk with Malachi Martin over dinner, simply enjoying his company, when he told us that he was once parachuted over some remote region, captured by an unfriendly militia, and subsequently subjected to physical torture. I have no recollection what exactly we were talking about that prompted this amazing disclosure, nor did we question Fr. Martin regarding the when, where and wherefore of that astounding chain of events. Taken aback by this revelation, and not realizing its critical importance to biographers, we did not pursue the matter beyond this point. Thea did go so far as to question Malachi Martin regarding the kind of torture he was subjected to, and he replied that it was "electrical shock to the genitals." Amazed if not dumbfounded, we returned to the preceding topic of conversation; and thus, alas, the subject was dropped.

There can obviously be no doubt that this incident pertains to that "period in Fr. Martin's life that is largely unknown, which is his work behind the Iron Curtain during the Cold War." It serves in fact to document quite conclusively that there *was* such a period. What, then, could have been the nature of that "work": what, in short, was his mission? I believe there can only be one answer, which in fact obtrudes itself: his mission, clearly, was *to ordain "underground" priests.* This explains its secrecy—the fact, for example, that he did not enter the Soviet domain by train or automobile as one normally does, but was parachuted into a remote region, evidently to make contact with elements of the Catholic underground. And it also explains why, having been captured by a Soviet militia, he was subsequently tortured: the purpose, quite obviously, must have been to extract information regarding "contact points" with the underground. The pieces of the puzzle are beginning to fit.

**If Fr. Martin was entrusted with the responsibility of ordaining priests behind the Iron Curtain, wouldn't he have been consecrated a bishop?**

If Malachi Martin was sent on a mission to ordain priests, it evidently follows that he *was in truth a bishop*. I myself became aware of this fact, first from his letters, which he invariably signed using the episcopal cross, which as one knows is the mark or emblem of episcopal rank. Moreover, on a number of occasions he gave us blessings which only a bishop can bestow. And lastly, when conversing about a certain "underground" priest, it happened that Malachi Martin—responding to something I had brought up—said to us: "If I had known this, I would not have laid my hands on him." He was of course referring to the ordination of that priest, at which he was present. Now clearly, the admission "I laid my hands" on a priest at his ordination can mean only one thing: it tells us that Malachi Martin was in fact one of the ordaining bishops.

One more question obtrudes itself: if Fr. Martin was indeed a bishop, why was this fact not known, why was it not officially acknowledged? Why in particular are there apparently no documents, no records in the appropriate archives to substantiate this fact? The explanation of this seeming incongruity resides evidently in the fact that Malachi Martin was consecrated, not to serve in a regular diocese, but precisely for the purpose of ordaining underground priests in regions behind the Iron Curtain: there was ample reason, thus, for secrecy. It all fits, and I myself have no further doubts in regard to this issue.

Given that Malachi Martin was ordained in 1954 and became private secretary to Cardinal Bea in 1958, one sees that his mission in Soviet-controlled territories must have taken place during that four-year interval, and thus when he was between 33 and 37 years of age—an appropriate time, it seems, for adventures of that kind. And might it not have been this unusual and heroic service to the Church that brought the young Jesuit to the personal attention of

7

the Pope and contributed to his extraordinary promotion in 1958, when Malachi Martin assumed one of the most coveted positions to which a cleric below Cardinal rank can aspire?

Finally, on the issue whether his experience "behind the Iron Curtain" might have played an important role in the formation of Malachi Martin's views regarding the crisis of modern civilization and of the Church, I am persuaded that such is undoubtedly the case. We know for a fact that what Our Lady has termed "the errors of Russia" have indeed spread all over the world, but few of us realize what actually stands at issue in this gargantuan onslaught. I surmise that Malachi Martin's encounters behind the Iron Curtain may have shed light upon this crucial issue: who knows whether his prophetic soul may have learned the secret directly from the eyes of his torturers. We must remember that Fr. Martin knew more about the "dark side" of the universe than probably any of his peers, and that in fact he was frequently "in contact" with the demonic realm in his capacity as an exorcist. Putting it all together, I am personally convinced that his face-to-face encounter with Soviet style communism undoubtedly added a depth-dimension to his understanding of the crisis presently afflicting both the Church and modern civilization at large which other observers of the contemporary scene do not possess.

**In his last years, Malachi Martin developed a relationship with Dr. Rama Coomaraswamy, a scholar of the post-Vatican II period of the Church. What information did Dr. Coomaraswamy make available that is critical to understanding the work of Fr. Martin?**

You have hit upon the one source, to my knowledge, which confirms the fact that Malachi Martin ordained priests for the underground Church in Russia, and that indeed he parachuted into Soviet-controlled territory; Dr. Coomaraswamy does so in a letter, dated June 7, 2002, addressed to Bishop Dolan—who apparently had made critical and misleading comments about Malachi Martin—a copy of which he sent me. It defends Fr. Martin against several of the false accusations raised against him from various sides, beginning with the Kaiser book.

The letter is valuable also on account of the picture it paints of this holy priest as a man of deep prayer—"without any ego" Coomaraswamy makes it a point to say—totally dedicated to the service of the true Church, which he perceived to be presently "going underground" somewhat as in the period before the time of Constantine. The letter ends with a reference to Dr. Coomaraswamy's last telephone conversation with Malachi Martin, which he had also referred to in a letter to me dated April 12, 2000. In the course of that conversation Fr. Malachi confided to his friend how that morning, while celebrating Mass, "he had been so totally one with Christ, so totally united with Him, as never before." After hanging up, the thought struck Coomaraswamy: "My God, he is ready to die!" And indeed, that very night he suffered his fatal stroke.

**What is the significance of the work of Malachi Martin? There has been much analysis of the present crisis of modern-day Catholicism. What is unique about Fr. Martin's analysis of this period? Do you think that Fr. Martin's various experiences played a crucial role in developing his analysis of the modern Church?**

I perceive Malachi Martin as the providential historian of the Roman Catholic Church in the present post-Vatican II era. No one else, so far as I can discern, has as deep a comprehension of the Council: its underlying causes, the devastation it has wrought and is continuing to inflict, and finally its overall function in the ultimate perfection of the Church. Others have perceived this or that facet—have, for example, lamented the secularization of doctrine, the vulgarization of the liturgy and the decline of authentic Catholic devotion—but when it comes to an understanding of the deep causes, and what could almost be termed the "necessity" of that horrific interlude, it appears that Malachi Martin stands alone in the depth, the expanse, and the clarity of his vision.

What I find unique in his analysis of this historical period is his understanding, in the first place, of the why and wherefore of the present ecclesial disintegration, and secondly, of the deep connection between what is happening in the Church and the major trends of western civilization at large; and while on the latter issue there may be others who have perceived at least parts or aspects of that connection, when it comes to the first—which is after all by far the most important issue—Malachi Martin seems to stand without a peer.

One can see in retrospect that all the multifarious experiences and achievements of his singularly rich and multifaceted life have qualified him eminently and uniquely for this role of historian *par excellence* of the present-day Catholic Church. I hesitate to recount the list of these experiences and achievements because it is so long and worthy of close examination. But to take at least a brief look: his story begins in Ireland, in a family and a culture deeply rooted in the authentic Catholic tradition. Here is where this man was formed and rendered Catholic to the bone, so that by the time he entered the Jesuit order at the age of eighteen, "Pater Sanctus Ignatius had captured my soul entirely" as he confided near the end of his life. Then came the doctorate in archeology, Oriental studies and Semitic languages, which opened a world to the young scholar about which most of us know almost nothing at all. And I might mention that it was precisely on the basis of insights gleaned from these sources that Malachi Martin could respond knowledgeably half a century later to issues I raised in my letters, and was able to transcend the customary limitations in that regard on the part of contemporary theologians. Then came the remarkable period of working for the underground Church behind the Iron Curtain, which as I have suggested before, doubtlessly deepened his understanding of the Soviet enterprise: of those "errors" in particular concerning which Our Lady of Fatima had warned the Conciliar popes. Following this, for a brief seven years, Malachi Martin found himself at the very center of that ecclesiastic hierarchy as a protégé of Pope John XXIII and Cardinal Bea: he had now attained to the coveted rank of a Vatican confidant, privy to just about all that transpired behind closed doors. And the result of that "insider" prerogative was, as we know, that he became thoroughly disillusioned with the existing status quo, to the point of asking to be released from the Jesuit order to exercise the humble ministry of a secular priest. Yet, despite this disassociation from the centers of ecclesial governance, he retained his connections in Rome and continued to keep himself abreast of all that was happening within the power centers not only of the Catholic Church, but of the secular world at large; for by now he had come to realize that the two are inextricably connected.

But there is more that needs to be said: for there is another realm—a dimension, if you will, normally closed to mankind—into which Malachi Martin was wont to penetrate: I am referring to what is properly termed the *angelic* realm, which itself breaks into two disparate domains. To begin with, he often alluded to his "two angels": it was from him that I learned that we all have not only a "guardian" angel, but a so-called "destiny" angel as well, assigned to us at conception and at birth respectively. And it seems that Malachi Martin had a rare gift to commune with both, which apparently he did on a daily basis. What is more, he also prayed daily to the entire angelic hierarchy right up to the Cherubim and Seraphim—a remarkable practice even for a priest, which cannot but have affected his powers of perception profoundly. One knows, moreover, that Malachi Martin likewise "conversed" with the fallen or demonic portion of the angelic realm in his capacity as an exorcist; and I personally have no doubt that from these nether sources as well he derived insights contributing their share to a global in-depth understanding of "the Church in the modern world." All told, I would say that when it comes to his well-nigh prophetic vision of what actually stands at issue in the social, political and ecclesiastic upheavals of our time, Malachi Martin seems to stand without a peer.

**Malachi Martin read the Third Secret of Fatima. Do you think that reading the Third Secret of Fatima contributed to his understanding of the crisis in the Church?**

Unfortunately, I never broached the subject of the Fatima revelation with Malachi Martin, nor did he ever refer to it. Yet I don't doubt for a moment that the message of Fatima—and of course especially the Third Secret—contributed decisively to his understanding of the crisis in the Church: after all, that cycle of Marian revelations constitutes arguably the key to the entire sequence of events initiated by Vatican II. Clearly, the Fatima messages constitute both a warning and a prophesy: a warning in effect to the Conciliar popes *not* to do what in fact they eventually did—despite, let me emphasize, having been thus forewarned by the Mother of God herself—and a prophesy concerning the calamitous consequences for the Church *and* the world that would ensue as a result. In regard to the Third Secret, there is reason to believe that it elaborates on a prophesy Our Lady had made half a century earlier at La Salette when she declared that "Rome will lose the faith and become the seat of the Antichrist."

Now, it seems to me that only in light of this horrendous revelation can we comprehend in depth Malachi Martin's outlook and mission in the Church. I surmise that the Fatima messages constitute in particular the ultimate basis for his unshakable conviction that the "institutional Church" is headed *irretrievably* towards dissolution: given Fr. Martin's profound and unflinching loyalty to what he reverentially termed the See of Peter, I surmise that nothing short of a revelation from the Mother of God herself could have made him "give up" on the present Vatican establishment.

But there is yet another side to the Fatima revelation that completes the picture and no doubt Malachi Martin's outlook as well. I am referring specifically to what Our Lady termed "the errors of Russia," which by now have presumably spread all over the world: what precisely are these "errors"? Is it simply a question of what we are wont to term "communism"? I surmise that what actually stands at issue is in fact tantamount to what Malachi Martin was wont to call "the New World Order." So far from a mere economic or political ideology, what confronts us here constitutes in reality a kind of religion: the religion of Antichrist to be precise. It was in his last book—which apparently he did not complete—that Malachi Martin put it all together under the stunning title: *"How the Institutional Catholic Church Became a Creature of the New World Order."* Here in a nutshell we have what strikes me as the definitive statement regarding the termination of the "institutional Church" we are witnessing today: *this is how "Rome becomes the seat of the Antichrist."*

**Part of the message of Fatima is a request by Our Lady for the Pope in union with the bishops of the world to consecrate Russia to her Immaculate Heart. Fr. Martin expressed the**
12

**view that salvation will come from the East, meaning Russia.
Do you believe that this view has merit?**

I did not know that Malachi Martin had expressed that view,
but can see from various directions why he might have reached
that conclusion. We should remember, first of all, that Russia has
had a very deep spiritual culture, extending from its priestly and
monastic ranks down to the humblest strata of society. That culture,
moreover, continued to flourish right through the nineteenth
century, undiminished by the gathering winds of rank materialism:
one needs but to recall such glorious names as that of St. Seraphim
of Sarov, St. Theophan the Recluse, or of the great staretz John of
Kronstadt, for instance, to glimpse the depths of the Russian soul.
That galaxy of towering followers of Christ includes moreover
men and women of the humblest rank, such as the lowly "pilgrim"
whose diaries created a sensation in the West. I find it regrettable
that the spiritual odyssey of this "hidden man of God"—leading
to the mystical depths of what in Orthodox tradition is termed
"prayer of the heart"—has received scant recognition among
Catholics.

I have long felt that the Roman Catholic and the Orthodox
halves of the Mystical Body need *desperately* to be rejoined: that
neither is complete without the other. It strikes me as unfortunate,
moreover, that Rome did not stretch out its hand *fraternally* to
its Eastern brethren till the post-Vatican II era, when it was in
a sense too late. I think we can agree that as the matter stands,
the sought-after reunification with the Russian Orthodox Church
cannot come about without divine assistance, which is to say
that in fact it can only be achieved through the intercession of
the Blessed Virgin herself. But as always, God asks something
in return: we are called upon to do our part. In this case it is the
Pope, in concert with the bishops of the world, that needs to obey
Our Lady's request by consecrating—not in fact "the world"—but
*Russia* specifically to her Immaculate Heart. This uncomplicated
act of faith and obedience—which so far has been spurned by the
reigning pontiffs—is apparently all it takes.

It should be noted that the Fatima message speaks—not
of "reunification"—but of a "conversion" on the part of Russia.
Now "conversion" has both a "from" and a "to", which we

should identify; and as regards the former, what needs to be discarded are not only the so-called "errors of Russia," but the offense of "schism" as well. There can be no doubt that Our Lady acknowledges the authentic Papacy, and insists that the Mystical Body, here on earth, requires a "visible head" representing her divine Son.

**The magazine *Christian Order* has stated that "controversy forever swirls around the late Father Malachi Martin." What do you think are the sources of this controversy?**

From the time Malachi Martin left the Jesuit order various and sundry charges were leveled against him from diverse quarters. The "defection" of a top-ranking Jesuit and Vatican insider, first of all, was itself bound to provoke recrimination. Add to this that his best-selling books and his numerous interviews disclosed facts that were, shall we say, "unflattering" to various segments of the reigning elite—how could this *not* provoke a response? To give but one example, let me recall his thinly-veiled disclosure, in *Vatican: A Novel*, that Pope John Paul I was indeed murdered, and in fact by a former Secretary of State! In short, no one should be surprised that Malachi Martin has been hounded by detractors and vilified; to which I would add that, as a representative of Christ, he *had to be* maligned.

There exists an entire literature accusing Fr. Martin of reprehensible conduct, along with a third-party counter-literature claiming to refute these accusations. As for Malachi Martin himself, he was far too busy writing books, hearing deathbed confessions and exorcising demons to respond to that "forever swirling" controversy. As he explained in a letter, he did not allow himself "to be diverted from fulfilling my mission as a priest and a servant of the Holy See of Peter."

**Do you think that Malachi Martin should be considered a servant of the See of Peter even though he was a critic of the Vatican?**

It seems to me that a true servant of the See of Peter is in fact *obligated* to be "a critic of the Vatican" when that institution becomes corrupt and succumbs to the seductions of Antichrist. I am of course aware of the time-honored Catholic mandate regarding submission to the Pope and the mortal danger of schism; yet I am convinced that, in the final count, *submission to the truth of Christ* trumps all. This does not mean, of course, that "every Tom, Dick, and Harry" can take it upon himself to render judgment upon issues of the faith normally adjudicated by papal authority: can in effect make himself a pope! Yet I am persuaded that there will always be men and women—even of humble rank—appointed in the providence of God to protect the Church from whatever assaults the enemy has contrived, to the end that the injury inflicted may not prove fatal. The divine commandment "Restore my Church" has doubtless been received and acted upon by many a chosen vessel throughout ecclesial history, failing which, I surmise, the Church might well have perished long ago.

My point, now, is that Malachi Martin was indeed such a chosen instrument of Christ. When, in the evening of his life, he confided that Pater Sanctus Ignatius had "captured my soul entirely," he was telling us that from the nineteenth year of his life onwards, he was in fact fully dedicated to the Jesuit mission, which consists above all in serving the Papacy. Even, therefore, when he levelled charges against the Conciliar popes, he did so in the service of the Holy See.

We should also remind ourselves that in the wake of the Fatima revelations our situation as Catholics has somewhat changed: we have been alerted—by the Mother of God herself— that all is not well in the Vatican, that in fact "Rome will lose the faith and become the seat of the Antichrist." And whereas obviously this revelation does not impact any fundamental dogma of the faith, it does clearly alter our existential connection with the current Vatican. I surmise, moreover, that where the present-day papacy fails, the Blessed Virgin herself steps in to guide and protect: that as never before in ecclesial history, the fate of the Church and the welfare of the faithful rests now squarely in her hands. To my mind at least, the best thing Pope John Paul II ever did was point to his rosary as if to say: *Here is your weapon; this is what will get you through!*

# Part II

## Science, Scientism and Christological Cosmology

**The next subject which I would like to cover is a book about Malachi Martin, entitled *In Quest of Catholicity*, which you have recently published. Could you tell us some basic facts about this book? Why did you have it published?**

The book, first of all, was not planned. I wrote to Malachi Martin as to a counselor to elicit his response regarding certain philosophic and theological tenets at which I had arrived. I should add that these tenets were based upon the recognition of a pre-Christian wisdom not generally shared by theologians but fully embraced, as it turned out, by Malachi Martin. Early in his life, when he was decoding paleontographic fragments antedating the Christian era, he became aware of the fact that there exists what he terms a "pre-Christian Christological knowledge." He came to realize, moreover, that facets of this supernatural wisdom could be found likewise in some of the principal pre-Christian traditions scattered around the globe. It thus turned out, to my great joy, that Malachi Martin concurred in the main with the philosophic and theological tenets I had expressed.

Upon re-reading my correspondence with Fr. Martin, seventeen years later, I was struck, first of all, by its remarkable coherence: the fact that while it covers a broad spectrum of topics, it yet seemed to cohere, seemed already in essence to constitute a *book*. You asked why I published that book: it was because I perceived its central message to be timely in the extreme. The point is not that it speaks to the ongoing crisis in the Catholic Church and of western civilization at large, but that it does so from a standpoint which rises above the current divide: in the words of Malachi Martin, it deblocks *"the impasse in which Roman Catholic intellectualism has been trapped these many years."*

What the book brings to light above all—its central message if you will—is that we presently stand in urgent need of that very "pre-Christian Christological knowledge" to which Malachi Martin alludes: that long-forgotten wisdom, the traces of which

16

he first encountered in his paleographic inquiries. It is the acknowledgment of that wisdom, precisely, that "deblocks the impasse" by opening the door to a vast domain of knowledge which for a very long time has been either ignored or ignorantly relegated to the realm of "pagan superstitions."

The question remains what is it precisely which renders that "pre-Christian Christological knowledge" imperative in our day; and the answer turns out to be simple: that long-forgotten knowledge is of a kind in which *theology and cosmology meet.* And let me add without delay that this constitutes by no means a lapse into pantheism but rather its very opposite: what that venerable wisdom offers—and what we desperately need—is a bona-fide *Christological cosmology.*

**Could you tell us why, in your view, such a meeting of theology and cosmology is needed to "deblock" the contemporary impasse?**

The reason is not hard to discern. It is abundantly apparent, after all, that ever since the so-called Enlightenment, the Catholic Church has been on the defensive vis-à-vis the scientific advance. The argument "You own the cosmos, we the supernatural" proves to be invalid, and only serves in the long run to undermine religious belief. Everyone understands that there has been an accelerating decline of faith in the supernatural, and that the scientific onslaught has had a profound effect upon the Catholic Church: is this not indeed in large measure what the Vatican II revolution was about? One needs but recall the frenzied adulation bestowed upon the person of Teilhard de Chardin to realize that his proposed synthesis of science and theology was, at the very least, a major driving force in the resultant overthrow of traditional Catholicism. The fact is that, in the name of what proved ultimately to be a "science-fiction" theology, major segments within the Catholic Church—up to the highest ranks!—have been led astray.

It needs to be recognized that a theology cannot stand alone, that in the long run it demands a concomitant cosmology. And that is something the pre-Conciliar Church did not possess: for this we need to go back all the way to what Malachi Martin calls "the pre-Christian Christological knowledge."

**You mentioned Teilhard de Chardin. Do you believe that Teilhard de Chardin is a significant figure in Church history?**

I believe more than that: I perceive Teilhard de Chardin to be the dominant theologian of the twentieth century, the one who inspired the proponents and aficionados of *la nouvelle theologie*: it was at bottom he that triumphed at the fateful Council which has radically altered the Church.

What is it, then, that renders his thought so powerful, so immensely attractive to Catholic intellectuals of our day? It is, first of all, the fact that he speaks in the hallowed name of Science: his theology is supposedly based, not on faith or metaphysical reasoning, but upon the hard facts of scientific discovery. And what precisely are these facts? At bottom, there is but one: and that is Evolution. To be sure, Teilhard accepts Darwin's theory lock, stock, and barrel; but he enlarges the concept immeasurably: he perceives evolution as a universal principle operative everywhere, and constituting the basis of all existing things. In fact, strictly speaking, there *are* no things; as Teilhard has put it with shocking clarity: "When all is said and done, Evolution is the first, the last, the only thing in which I believe." Others have extended the notion from biology to various spheres, such as the social or the intellectual, but Teilhard alone has taken the ultimate step: he has actually *deified* the concept. Evolution has *de facto* become his God. Now, such a claim can only be one of two things: it must be either a case of sheer madness or indeed of prophesy—and I find it unfortunate that Catholic intellectuals have, by a huge margin, opted for the latter alternative. Evolution with a capital E has in fact become the Leitmotif of virtually all *modern* theology; like the underlying drone in Indian music, it is ever present, whether we hear it or not.

Let us note, moreover, that what Teilhard offers an astonished and thirsting Catholic world is indeed a *Christological cosmology*: that is precisely what his "scientific" theology purports to be. It is moreover the only thing a theology *can be*, given that it *is* "scientific." But as should *de jure* be apparent to every scientifically literate person, it *is not*: if even classical Darwinism proves to be indefensible on scientific ground, so all the more is the Teilhardian extrapolation, the key terms of which have in fact no scientific

18

sense at all. I find it truly amazing that top-ranking theologians of the Catholic Church could have so readily succumbed to what is indeed quite literally a science-fiction theology.

There is so much to be said on this (to me) fascinating subject—I have written an entire book on Teilhard de Chardin as you know—that I need to stop myself from breaking the "conversational" format of this interview. One more point, however, I must not neglect to mention: there is in the case of Teilhard de Chardin a demonstrable demonic connection which can be traced to a kind of "mystical experience" to which Teilhard alludes in an early composition, published in 1919. It speaks in dramatic terms of an encounter with a being described as "equivocal, turbid, the combined essence of all evil and all goodness," which fastened itself upon him: "And now I am established on you for life, or for death" the Thing declares. I regret very much that I never thought of asking Malachi Martin about this remarkable and almost universally unnoticed episode; all I can say is that to me it savors of demonic possession. And most assuredly, that would go a long way to explain the enormity of the Teilhardian influence, its decisive impact upon the Catholic scene at the exact moment when the reigning popes perpetrated their act of disobedience to the Mother of God. Is it then by way of Teilhard de Chardin that "Rome" became a habitat of Antichrist? I believe that in a way it was.

**The question arises, of course, how the authentically Christological cosmology squares with contemporary scientific findings. Could you say a few words regarding this issue?**

In point of fact the Christological cosmology does "square" with contemporary scientific findings, so long as we distinguish sharply between scientific fact and scientistic fiction, a discrepancy which however is rarely discerned.

Let me point out, first of all, that strictly speaking modern science has produced no cosmology, and is in fact incapable—by virtue of its very methodology—of doing so. Unbeknownst even to most scientists, however, it compensates for this deficiency by projecting various cosmological claims *as if* they were scientifically authorized. Take the case of physics, the foundational science:

physicists have convinced themselves as well as the public at large that the universe is made up simply of fundamental particles. But trust me: there never has been, nor *can there be*, a scientific proof of this so-called fact. Quite to the contrary: there are rigorously valid grounds for concluding that *perceptible* objects (from chunks of rock to scientific instruments) do *not* in fact reduce to an ensemble of quantum particles; as I have shown in a monograph, the so-called measuring problem—which has stymied physicists since around 1925—demands no less.

But whereas contemporary science has produced no bona-fide cosmology, it has imposed a kind of pseudo-cosmology, masquerading as science, upon an unsuspecting public, based upon the aforesaid claim that the universe—and all it contains—is "made up of quantum particles and nothing more." It is the resultant conglomerate of pseudo-scientific notions, proclaimed under the banner of science, that has in time befuddled the public at large, and has moreover impacted a great many of our churchmen to the point of driving them literally to the brink of apostasy. Now, even as truth alone remedies error, so genuine cosmology constitutes likewise the one and only effective antidote to the current plague of scientistic belief. And that is why we stand today in need—in *desperate* need—of an authentically *Christological* cosmology.

One more point should be made to round out the picture: not only does that authentic cosmology neutralize and dispel the scientistic illusions of our day, but it fulfills a second vital function; for it happens that on the basis of the genuinely Christological cosmology one can understand the actual discoveries of science—of quantum physics, for example—*ontologically* by integrating them into that larger picture: that perennial doctrine, which derives not simply from human imagination or genius, but indeed from Christ Himself.

**Is the fundamental problem of modern man that he has accepted a scientific worldview that does not allow for a belief in a supernatural religion?**

First of all, let me point out that modern man has not in fact accepted a "scientific" worldview at all; his Weltanschauung is actually *scientistic*, which is to say that it purports to be scientific—to be based upon sound scientific evidence—whereas in truth it is not. This is a matter I have dealt with at great length and in full rigor; though almost universally unrecognized these days, it is indeed a fact that in the name of science modern man has been profoundly—and dangerously!—misled.

You are no doubt right in suggesting that this scientistic worldview excludes belief in a supernatural religion. Actually, however it excludes not only the supernatural, but quite literally the better half of the natural as well. The explanation of this rather surprising fact hinges upon the categorical distinction—one of the most penetrating, I believe, in all of philosophy—between *quantities* and *qualities*, the point being that the scientistic Weltanschauung has "categorically" excluded the latter from its purview. And this entails a second fact, perhaps more startling even than the first: it happens that no one consistently believes the so-called scientific worldview, that in fact even the greatest scientist *disbelieves* it in his daily life. My point is that we normally take the grass to be *green*, even though—in our "scientific" moments—we staunchly maintain that it is not. The almost universally unnoticed fact is that we, denizens of the modern age, have been unwittingly plunged into a state of collective schizophrenia, a condition scarcely compatible with authentic sanity.

Yet there is more; for it happens that *qualities* and *quantities* are not on a par: metaphysically speaking, qualities derive "from above" whereas quantities stem from what might be termed the nadir of the integral cosmos. Of course, this fact has become incomprehensible to modernized mankind; along with the concept of qualities we have lost the idea of *verticality*: in the scientistic cosmos there is no more "above," and for that matter, no more "below" as well. It is ironic that a civilization which despises the notion of a "flat Earth" should have fallen prey to the incomparably greater illusion of a "flat cosmos"!

But getting back to your question: yes, the "scientific" worldview does indeed exclude the supernatural—along with the song of birds, the roar of breaking waves, and in fact all that constitutes the very *essence* of this world, let alone what speaks to us of "higher" realms.

**Some of the content of the intellectual discussions covered in your conversations with Malachi Martin are difficult for many readers to understand. Is it necessary for a reader to follow all the details of the intellectual discussions to learn something from your book? What do these intellectual discussions reveal about the person of Malachi Martin?**

I certainly agree with you that some of what is said in my letters to Malachi Martin as well as in his responses may be difficult to understand, to the point of being well-nigh incomprehensible to the average reader. Yet, on the other hand, most of the interchange does not pertain to that category, and should be of interest to a broad spectrum of readers seeking to better understand what is presently happening within the Catholic Church and in western civilization at large. And even when it comes to the more demanding portion of the discourse, I presume the discerning non-specialist may well pick up something of the gist.

As to what these discussions reveal about the person of Malachi Martin, I would say that they disclose a side of him which one has not seen before. We have witnessed the historian and novelist shedding light upon the course of historical events, and we have caught a glimpse of the priest guiding his flock in the path of Catholic tradition; what we have *not* seen in him before, on the other hand, is the indicator of truths beyond the bounds of dogmatic theology: of doctrines namely which might properly be characterized as "esoteric." Never before, so far as I can tell, did Malachi Martin allude to an "*impasse in which Roman Catholic intellectualism has been blocked these many years,*" much less refer to a non-Catholic mystic of the seventeenth century as "*a very Holy Spirit enlightened man destined by Christ the Revelator of God's mystery to indicate to us of the latter days... how we can fill out our understanding of God.*" The very notion that the pre-Conciliar teaching was yet somehow incomplete, that there was space left in our "knowledge of God" that needed to be "filled out"—by someone outside the institutional Church no less—all this is brand new, and will no doubt come as a shock to many believing Catholics. It should be noted in this connection that in one of his letters Malachi Martin expresses the remarkably interesting view that notwithstanding its disastrous immediate effects, which he impugned unreservedly, Vatican II may yet in the long run fulfill a useful and indeed necessary function, which is "*to facilitate the sense of the esoteric,*" a category which apparently he identified with what he termed "*the mystical knowledge of the divine as distinct from the rational.*"

Lastly, let me point out why these revelations were given, so to speak, in private, and are nowhere to be found in his previously published writings or public statements issued during his lifetime. The reason for this silence is in fact rather evident: these disclosures, seemingly beyond the pale of "catechetical orthodoxy," would no doubt have disturbed devout and aspiring constituents of his flock, believing Catholics whom he was eager to help and to edify. Yet even so it emerges from his correspondence that he believed the time to be close at hand when it shall be needful for the Church at large to open her purview to that level of "*mystical knowledge*" which does indeed "*exceed the rational.*" As I observed in the Introduction to the book, Malachi Martin had his eye not only on the Church that was, but also—and perhaps above all—on the Church that is to be, when she shall rise from the darkness of the present Entombment to the splendor of her Resurrection.

**Malachi Martin was a staunch traditional Catholic, yet in his writings, such as in the book *The Decline and Fall of the Roman Church*, he sometimes was critical of the actions of pre-Conciliar churchmen. Is this not a contradiction?**

I perceive no contradiction whatsoever in that regard, all the more since, as you stipulate, Malachi Martin's criticism applies specifically to "the *actions* of pre-Conciliar churchmen." Happily, no one has ever suggested that churchmen—including popes—are invariably saints! The truth of the matter is that not a few were rather bad hombres, to put it mildly.

I am glad you mentioned *The Decline and Fall of the Roman Church*: a masterpiece of historical scholarship which moreover makes for a fascinating read. Here Malachi Martin—in full possession of his literary genius—presents us with vignettes depicting memorable events of papal history, covering the entire moral spectrum: literally from the heights of sainthood to the depths of villainy and depravity. I will never forget—on the side of the saints—the picture of Leo the Great, seated on his mule, advancing toward the southern shore of the river Po to stare down Attila the Hun, accompanied only by a group of monks singing psalms. On the opposing shore, arrayed against him, waits Attila on his steed, backed by a sea of mounted Huns holding lances with "a rotting human head" impaled thereon. An unforgettable scene! We must remember: in that encounter, that contest in the year 452 AD between *spiritual* and raw earthly might, the fate of Christendom—and indeed of western civilization at large—hung in the balance. One hardly need say more regarding the glory of the papacy!

Yet there is however another side that needs likewise to be told, and Malachi Martin rises to the occasion both as a historian and a literary master. Where there is a zenith there is also perforce a nadir, which in papal history is perhaps realized most amply in the person of Pope Boniface VIII, whose story—replete with treachery, murders, massacres and vileness of virtually every description—Malachi Martin relates accurately, eloquently, and without flinching. And so it should be: I cannot imagine that Christ would have it any other way. After all, He himself provides the example *par excellence* of "calling a spade a spade."

I think your question is suggestive of an important point: there is a right and a wrong way of "respecting" the popes, and it is nowadays more needful than ever before to discern the difference: the Francis pontificate is hardly the time for simple-minded papolatry!

**I do wish to cover one of the intellectual topics that you discussed with Malachi Martin. You had an exchange of letters with Fr. Martin concerning Dr. Catherine Pickstock, who spoke at a conference sponsored by the traditional Catholic movement. What is the significance of the work of Dr. Catherine Pickstock?**

It was Malachi Martin who alerted me to the work of Catherine Pickstock. He was at the time reading her book—her Cambridge doctoral dissertation—which had just been published under the intriguing title: *After Writing: On the Liturgical Consummation of Philosophy*. What can I say? The book is a masterpiece, a breakthrough without precedent in recent history. After deconstructing Derridean postmodernism to the point where virtually nothing remains, she launches into an analysis of Plato's *Phaedrus* which takes one's breath away, and goes on to scrutinize the evolution of Western thought from a point of vantage all her own. Even her use of language is inimitably her own—and erudite to such a degree that Malachi Martin himself, that master of the English tongue, was obliged not infrequently to consult a dictionary.

What primarily concerns us is of course the depth of understanding Catherine Pickstock conveys; and it is in this regard that she displays a degree of mastery not seen within our academic ranks for a very long time. Everything she sets her gaze upon is cast in a new light; even as her language is inimitable and unique, so is her thought. Whether she speaks of Duns Scotus or of Martin Heidegger, her discourse invariably breaks new ground and attains hitherto unimagined depths. What fascinated me the most, however, is her insight into *liturgy* and what might be termed the "liturgical dimension" of human culture. Above all, under this rubric, I should refer to her extensive commentary on the Tridentine rite of Mass, which she teaches us to look upon, literally, with new eyes, giving us to understand—as the subtitle of her book apprises us—that *here*, precisely, philosophy as such attains its consummation!

It should not surprise us that this philosophical revolution impacts in particular our comprehension of Thomism—the authentic doctrine of the Angelic Doctor himself—profoundly: in this regard as well Catherine Pickstock has broken new ground. One might say that she has in fact de-Aristotelianized that philosophy by unearthing its Platonist roots. She does so by reflecting in depth upon the *esse/essentia* dichotomy to demonstrate the categorical primacy of *esse*: of *being* as inseparable from God. The fact is that this absolutely fundamental recognition casts everything in a new light—"disturbs prior categories" as she puts it rather modestly—and reveals a metaphysics that vastly exceeds what we take to be Thomistic. For my part I surmise that Catherine Pickstock has succeeded in bringing to light—after perhaps some seven hundred years of virtual oblivion—what might indeed be termed the "esoteric core" of Thomistic philosophy. I cannot but perceive this, moreover, as no less than a providential occurrence pointing to a renaissance of the Catholic Church, what Malachi Martin calls her Resurrection.

**Some traditional Catholic intellectuals believe that Dr. Catherine Pickstock's insights strengthen the case for the traditional liturgy. Do you believe that this view is correct?**

I do, most emphatically, regard this view to be correct, but would add that Catherine Pickstock has not only "strengthened the case for the traditional liturgy," but has given us a glimpse of what liturgy actually *is*. What stands at issue is a *metaphysical* comprehension which the post-Vatican II "reformers of the liturgy" evidently did not possess: so long as one entertains a fallacious view of the cosmos—of "space, time, and matter" if you will—one simply cannot grasp the very "point" of the authentic liturgy, which in a manner beyond human conception overcomes our foundational dichotomies, such as "here" and "there," "before" and "after," and so forth without end. Above all, the authentic rite of Mass breaks the dichotomy of "transcendent" and "immanent," and in so doing elevates us *liturgically* above the schism resulting from the Fall.

But who in the present post-Enlightenment era has even the foggiest notion regarding matters of this kind! If the "Fathers of Vatican II" had understood what in fact the sacred liturgy *is*, metaphysically speaking, they surely could not have "reformed" it right out of existence. At their hands the rite of Mass has become something essentially "nonliturgical," describable in large measure as a "celebration of man"—the very creature which, in the authentic rite, is virtually extinguished, that is to say, *transcended*.

There may have been some merit in the post-Conciliar call for a *resourcement*—but what the *periti* in question apparently failed to grasp is that the times of nascent Christianity—what might perhaps be termed the *liturgical* era—have become for us a closed book. In fact, as Catherine Pickstock points out, the worshipping Christian community itself was then in a profound sense "liturgical," a condition which could perhaps be readily described as the diametric opposite of most contemporary congregations: those multitudes of "red-blooded" individuals persuaded of their "inalienable rights" and near-perfect state proclaimed from Catholic pulpits for the past half century.

I should add that the profound incomprehension of liturgy *per se* on the part of the reforming *periti* did not originate abruptly with the Council, but has a history going back a good many centuries, and is no doubt intimately connected with the effective disappearance or exclusion of what I have referred to earlier as the "esoteric core" of Thomism. The fact is that an "Aristotelianized" Thomism is inherently incapable of grasping the very essence of authentic liturgy, which as I have said, transcends our dichotomies and culminates in the mystery of "transubstantiation." On the other hand, the subtitle of Catherine Pickstock's treatise, so far from constituting a literary embellishment, is indeed expressive of the fact that authentic liturgy does in truth realize that supernal wisdom of which authentic philosophy is the quest. And one might add that the main title—*After Writing*—affirms the same: the fact, namely, that the "ultimate metaphysics" cannot be "written down," cannot be "mentally" grasped, but can only be experienced by way of the liturgical act in which, as Catherine Pickstock explains, "the occurrence of the impossible" is realized through the mediation of Christ.

**You alluded at the outset to your disappointment with academic philosophy as a student at Cornell University: in your own words, you concluded then that "philosophy is dead." And now you so highly extoll an academic philosopher of our time! Can you resolve that seeming contradiction?**

To begin with, let me say a few more words regarding my experience at Cornell. By the time I entered as a freshman I had read enough and thought enough to realize that philosophy constitutes *de jure* a sacred quest, which as such must engage—not just the rational intellect—but the whole man. I don't know just how I came to hold this view, but surmise that it was not in fact derived from an external source. There is much, I believe,

27

that every human being brings with him at birth: we do not arrive in this world as a *tabula rasa*. In any case, my conception of philosophy as a "sacred quest" was obviously *not* shared by the faculty at Cornell, who for the most part seemed to believe that philosophy has more to do, ultimately, with language than with reality.

I am not much given to relating biographical anecdotes, but let me share with you an incident that speaks to the issue at hand. Having accepted a graduate fellowship in the Department of Philosophy at Cornell, I duly presented myself to begin studies for a Ph.D. One of our assignments during the first semester was to read Kant's *Critique of Pure Reason* from cover to cover, along with Norman Kemp Smith's commentary thereon, which was almost as voluminous. Pondering this literature, it did not take me long to conclude that these Kantian ratiocinations, brilliant though they may be, have little to do with that *Sophia*—that more-than-human Wisdom—of which authentic philosophy, by its very designation, is literally the *love*. And so, three weeks into the semester, I resigned my fellowship and left Cornell University.

I had always been attracted to the natural world, to forests and mountains especially; and so I resolved to proceed to the great Northwest, henceforth to earn my keep as a lumberjack. No doubt I had an unrealistic and overly romanticized conception of what this entails; but in any case, at that point fate abruptly intervened. I had made my intentions known to my brother, who at the time was studying chemical engineering at Purdue University. He immediately proceeded to the chairman of the physics department to tell him about my case, going so far as to put my letter in his hands. The verdict was instant: "Tell your brother to present himself in my office Monday morning to assume his duties as a teaching assistant." It seems the voice of Providence had spoken: despite my very mixed feelings regarding the contemporary academic world, I was destined to pass most of my professional life in its precincts—but *not* in departments of philosophy! Meanwhile I have found no reason to change my outlook regarding the state of that discipline: I surmise that academic philosophy today is still every bit as "dead" as it was when I made my exodus from Cornell half a century ago.

28

The case of Catherine Pickstock strikes me as the exception that proves the rule; her philosophy—which meets the highest standards and leaves me speechless—is to be seen, I surmise, as the iconic "white spot" in the black field. I should add that her mentor at Cambridge University, Professor John Milbank, is the founder of a movement termed "radical orthodoxy," which likewise breaks the confines of the contemporary philosophic mold. It may be—*Deo volente*—that we are witnessing the approaching end of the era ushered in by the Enlightenment: the decisive breakthrough signaling a rebirth of authentic philosophy. One can certainly hope that such is the case; but as yet we cannot be certain. I personally incline to believe that this rebirth will come more or less at the moment in history when the Blessed Virgin shall intervene to terminate the "satanic disorientation" presently afflicting the Catholic Church: when She will *"crush the serpent's head"*—but time will tell.

**You spoke earlier of the discrepancy between "scientific fact" and "scientistic fiction." Could you perhaps tell us to what degree there is an awareness of that discrepancy—that perilous deception—within the academic ranks?**

One needs first of all to distinguish between various scientific domains. When it comes to the fundamental science, which is physics, it is safe to say that the distinction between fact and fiction to which I refer is nowhere discerned: the recognition that a fundamental distinction is to be made between the *physical* universe—the universe as conceived by the physicist—and the *corporeal* which we perceive with our senses, appears to have zero currency in physics departments throughout the western world. Although, in a monograph devoted to the issue, I have proved with full rigor that this *ontological* discernment between the physical and the corporeal is not only consistent with what physics by its very *modus operandi* is able to ascertain, but in fact resolves the seeming paradoxes of quantum theory—it appears that in this regard nothing as yet has changed. Physics professors at large continue to espouse philosophic premises discredited long ago, while regarding themselves to be "hard-headed empiricists": it is almost as if the uncanny precision exemplified in their scientific pursuit were compensated by a naïve amateurism when it comes to the philosophic domain.

Getting back to the "science fiction" issue: when it comes to the biological sciences—not to speak of the psychological, which arguably are not sciences at all—the case is not as clear-cut. What mainly stands at issue is the Darwinist theory of evolution: the question whether this central tenet constitutes indeed a scientific fact. And here it turns out that professional opinions are nowadays divided: not equally, to be sure, but nonetheless significantly. Since roughly the middle of the twentieth century a growing number of scientists have defected from the official stance. The word is out that there is actually no bona-fide scientific evidence in support of Darwin's conjecture, and that in fact, with the advance of the biological sciences, especially on the molecular level, contrary evidence has been piling up. It thus appears, in contradiction to the official claim, that the Darwinist tenet is in truth upheld on *a priori* ideological grounds. What is more, that fateful hypothesis is being aggressively imposed, in the name of science, first upon the scientific community itself, and thence upon society, upon civilization at large. Let me emphasize that in point of fact the individual scientist is by no means free to think and to publish as he wills. Yet, despite the imperative to uphold what is doubtless the central dogma of the reigning status quo—on pain of ostracism or dismissal—defections on the part of scientists do occur, as I have said, and the dissenting ranks are in fact beginning to swell. It is not entirely inconceivable that a so-called change of paradigm may yet be forced upon an adamantly recalcitrant scientific community somewhere down the road.

What needs to be grasped is that the contemporary scientific enterprise is by no means the "disinterested" quest for truth it is reputed to be, but in fact is driven by deeply-rooted commitments of an ideological kind: the materialism and moral relativism which "comes out" so to speak is indeed what has powered the modern-day scientific enterprise virtually from its inception. The public at large is of course awed into submission by the marvels of technology which today surround us on all sides—the veritable *"signs and wonders that could deceive even the elect"*—which however do not, even in the slightest degree, corroborate the scientistic tenets one mistakes almost universally for scientific truth.

But whereas by right our universities should lead the way in the detection of scientistic fallacy, they actually serve in fact to perpetuate that upside-down Weltanschauung and befuddle the public all the more. There are, to be sure, counter-currents as we have noted, beginning with honest biologists risking expulsion; yet even so the partisans of the status quo remain to this day solidly in command within the academic establishment.

**A Canadian newspaper columnist, Terence Corcoran, once wrote that public policy is being made of the claims of what he calls junk science. Do you think this opinion is correct?**

I think it is partially correct. There certainly is such a thing as "junk science," and there can be no doubt that in certain instances—conceivably, for example, in the case of "climate change"—it can have a significant impact upon public policy.

The effect of junk science, however, is miniscule compared to two other factors associated with the scientific enterprise: technology obviously, and scientism. It is by way of these two "offspring" that science dominates our civilization, whereas its direct impact upon society is by comparison insignificant, due to the fact that only a relatively small segment of the population has any authentic knowledge of what science itself has to say. This of course holds true above all for the physical sciences, which in a way underlie the rest: these disciplines, by virtue of being incurably mathematical, are comprehended by very few.

**Has science in some fields evolved into an alternative religion, where scientific theories are held as dogmas and open inquiry is not encouraged? For example, any scientist who challenges Darwin's theory of evolution is immediately dismissed as a crank.**

The idea of evolution occupies no doubt a special place in the scientific domain and carries the potential of religious arrogation. For that matter, numerous other conceptions do so as well, but not to the same degree. We must remember that man is indeed

31

by nature "religious": created to worship, he can hardly abstain from doing so. If therefore he fails to worship the true God, he is prone to adore some idol in His stead—for instance "Liberty," "Fraternity," or yes, "Evolution." Even the banal qualifies: even "climate change" has its clericals! But despite the unlimited scope of things to idolize, there is something special about "evolution"— presumably because it can be viewed *à la* Teilhard de Chardin as the Creator of all things. To be precise, that "Evolution" with a capital E constitutes in fact an *inversion* of God, betokening its satanic inspiration: for whereas the true God creates all things in the *nunc stans* of eternity, Teilhard's "God of Evolution" is said to create in time over millions of years, and in the final count to change—to be "endomorphized"—himself.

You asked whether science has evolved an alternative religion. I believe it has: an ensemble of religions, in fact. And yet it could be argued that in this pantheon of "gods," there is a central figure, which by now has manifested its hegemony: and it should surprise no one that this is in fact none other than the very "god of Evolution" Teilhard confessed to be "the first, the last, the only thing in which I believe."

**You speak of an ideology that drives the contemporary scientific enterprise. Would you say that this ideology is basically anti-Christian? Do you think that anti-Christian ideas have pervaded the thinking of scientists in the modern scientific community?**

I believe that the ideology which powers the scientific enterprise is indeed anti-Christian in its roots as well as in its impact upon western society. In its roots means in its origin, in the spirit which inspires and drives that ideology, which strictly speaking is not rational or ratiocinative and must therefore be inherently *angelic*. And this leaves us with *two* generic possibilities; for as we know from the teaching of Christ: *"He that is not with me is against me."*

This does not mean, of course, that everyone who has succumbed to the scientistic worldview is *ipso facto* possessed by evil spirits: if that were the case, one wonders how many individuals would be left standing! But happily this is not the case. One must remember, in the case of Christians, that almost all have been affected by scientistic tenets in various degrees, and that, in particular, the greater part of the Catholic hierarchy these days is in fact deeply immersed in scientism, to the point of reinterpreting doctrines of the Church in light of scientistic notions. The classic example and reigning paradigm, of course, is Teilhard de Chardin, who went so far as to construct a new religion—"a better Christianity" he called it—on scientistic grounds.

One should also recall that scientism comes in various forms and guises, and that it is needful in particular to distinguish the physical from the biological or Darwinist kind. For whereas just about everyone accepts the former—the notion, for instance, that corporeal objects are "made of" fundamental particles—the Christian communities have become quite sharply divided over the question of Darwinism. It might not in fact be too much of an exaggeration to suggest that it is this issue, fundamentally, that separates the traditional Catholic from the post-Conciliar in point of worldview: for what indeed characterizes the post-Conciliar Church is the fact that, in this respect at least, it is inherently Teilhardian.

The impact of scientism, moreover, does not stop at the level of a worldview, but in time affects all values and beliefs; and whereas scientism and Christian faith can no doubt coexist for a time, this union is evidently precarious and unsustainable in the long run. The two competing forces are in truth irreconcilably opposed—remember: *"He that is not with me is against me"*—and in the end, one or the other is bound to prevail.

The crucial fact is that, as Christians, we are not at liberty to accept a worldview fundamentally at odds with the teaching of Christ. Even though "scientism" is not listed in our catechisms under the rubric of "sin", it is nonetheless profoundly deleterious to the Christian life. I am reminded in this connection of a book, written by a priest, Fr. Felix Sarda y Salvany, entitled *"Liberalism is a Sin"*: even though I have yet to read that book, I doubt not that the good Padre was onto something real. And if *liberalism* be indeed a sin, so most assuredly is *scientism*: for the two are evidently animated by the same spirit and tend eventually to the same end. One might add, from an historical point of view, that as the twin offspring of the Enlightenment, *liberalism* and *scientism* are in fact inseparably connected—and we will leave it at that.

## Is the New World Order which is gradually being implemented an anti-Christian one?

Quite frankly, I am rather uncertain as to what actually confronts us on a human plane in the so-called New World Order. Is it a secret society, perhaps freemasonry with its thirty-three degrees? Or could it be simply a network of megalomaniac billionaires seeking to control world markets? Yet in spite of such uncertainty, I have no doubt regarding the *ultimate* protagonist of this movement, this "evolution," if you will, towards a globally omnipotent bureaucracy. After all, we clearly see its effect upon human culture in an institution such as the European Union, which has deprived the nations caught in its net of their very self-identity. Whatever the economic and possibly other benefits may be, such "globalization" cannot but result in enslavement and dehumanization, a scenario which as such carries the mark of Antichrist.

Happily—and at long last!—a counter-movement is emerging, beginning with Brexit in the U.K., followed by the Trump revolution in the U.S. What stands at issue here is not a question simply of economics—let alone a growing distaste for "political correctness"—but something far deeper, which perhaps the protagonists of the revolt do not themselves fully grasp. The key to the enigma, I surmise, is to be found in the Fatima revelation—inclusive of Quito and La Salette—which alerts us to the fact that a contest of apocalyptic magnitude is beginning to play out. When the "institutional Catholic Church" becomes—for a time!—"a Creature of the New World Order" as Malachi Martin informed us, what else could it be?

**Is the Church of Pope Francis actually developing into an anti-Church because it is going against the Church's traditions? In the end, will we have a secular new world order alongside a like-minded humanistic Church which, as Fr. Martin said, has**

**as its aim the building of man's habitat on earth rather than saving souls?**

As regards to the Church of Pope Francis, I think there can be little doubt that this institution is well on the way to becoming an anti-Church. One might argue that actually it has already been converted into "a like-minded humanistic" institution, Malachi Martin's "Creature of the New World Order." It seems to me Pope Francis himself announced the fact quite openly when he issued his encyclical on "global warming": that poster-child of the socio-economic Novus Ordo! Or again, was he not speaking as such a "creature" when he meddled in U.S. politics by campaigning in effect against Trump with his advice to "build bridges rather than walls"? It seems not to bother this Bishop of Rome in the least that Europe is fast losing its self-identity while absorbing populations hostile to Christianity and Judeo-Christian culture at large. Turning to theology, I would say that this subject is hardly a top priority with Francis. Though manifestly disinclined to enter into authentic theological discourse, he not infrequently quotes isolated fragments of scriptural text when these can be interpreted in support of his left-wing agenda, apparently to convey the impression that his "God of surprises" is fully on board.

I doubt however that such a "like-minded humanistic Church" can long endure. The path pursued in the wake of Vatican II, it seems to me, is not in fact a building up of something new, but the liquidation, rather, of an institution that is very old. I incline to surmise, moreover, that this dissolution—so far from constituting an unmitigated tragedy—may yet in the long-run serve a salutary end. True enough: the Church of Pope Francis has visibly joined forces with the "brave new world" in the project of "building man's habitat on earth"; but that project too is bound eventually to fail. Like the famous Tower of Babel, it is destined to collapse, and sooner perhaps than one might think. As Christians, we know this perfectly well, and as Catholics we know too what is to follow. As Our Lady apprises us: *My Immaculate Heart will triumph in the end.* Let us never forget—even for a moment!—*the final Victory belongs to Christ.*

**Have you written on the subject of the relationship between science and faith? What were your findings on this very broad subject?**

I don't recall having written explicitly on that question; but having long ago perceived the necessity of purging our contemporary Weltanschauung of its addiction to scientistic fantasies, I have dealt repeatedly and at length with the relation between scientific fact and scientistic beliefs. Yet once that basic distinction has been made clear, the relationship between science and faith can be readily grasped. The point is simple enough: whereas authentic science augments and strengthens our Christian faith by revealing the infinite Wisdom and Goodness of God, scientism has exactly the opposite effect: its implicit denial of transcendence replaces God in effect by a mental construct void of truth.

By way of comparison let me recall the much-maligned Ptolemaic cosmography, immortalized by Dante, with its concentric spheres spreading outwards up to the so-called Empyrean, following which they *converge* towards *the throne of God.* Admittedly, what stands "above" the Empyrean escapes our current scientific purview and can only be described in symbolic terms; the point, however, is that the recognition of that Boundary saves us from error: from idolatry no less. One can even say more: the Ptolemaic cosmography as envisaged by Dante penetrates beyond our material world by availing itself of a language—a symbolism, one can say—which, by virtue of being predominantly *qualitative*, escapes from the bounds to which every worldview of a *quantitative* kind is subject *ipso facto*: by the very fact, namely, that it *is* quantitative. We, denizens of the modern world, have in large measure lost the gift of direct sight, the ability of penetrating symbols—of "reading the icon" as the Orthodox might say; and in virtue of this attrition we have become confined to a spatio-temporally bounded universe, what the poet calls "this narrow world," which is indeed destined one day to disappear "and leave not a wreck behind."

It is ironic that contemporary astrophysics regales us with its billions of light years—as if to make up, in terms of sheer quantity, for the veritable infinity that perforce escapes the purview of our physical sciences by virtue of their *modus operandi*, which entails the exclusion of all *qualities*, of everything in fact that cannot be caught in their net of measurement. I should add parenthetically that our current "big bang" model of the four-dimensional universe is at bottom Darwinism on a cosmic scale, and like the original Darwinist hypothesis, is founded upon an unproved and indeed unprovable assumption: the so-called Copernican principle. As I have made clear in my writings, contemporary astrophysics is not, strictly speaking, a branch of physics, but constitutes once again an ideology-driven extrapolation ultimately void of scientific validity.

**You refer to "the Ptolemaic cosmography." Now most of us have been taught to believe that this cosmography has been disproved once and for all by Galileo and his scientific successors. How do you respond to this claim?**

First of all, let me speak to what one generally takes to be the central issue: the question of geocentrism. Almost everyone believes that Galileo was right—and the Church was wrong—in the famous dispute which in a way marks the birth of modern science and inaugurates the period historians refer to as the Enlightenment. Yet, actually, it turns out that the facts declare otherwise. The main point of contention at the Galileo trial, let us recall, was whether it is the Sun or the Earth that "moves." The Church, in keeping with the literal interpretation of Biblical texts and the Ptolemaic cosmography, insisted that the Sun rotates around a central and immobile Earth, whereas Galileo asserted—on what he believed to be scientific grounds—that the opposite holds true. Soon enough, moreover, the world at large sided with Galileo, in compliance with the belief—the modernist axiom—that "science has spoken, the case is closed." It may therefore come as a surprise to many that almost three centuries after the Galileo trial, in 1887 to be exact, when two physicists, named Michelson and Moreley, set about to measure the orbital velocity of the Earth in its annual revolution around the Sun, they found that this velocity *is in fact zero*. To be sure, that finding—which was scarcely publicized!— sent shock waves through the scientific communities, and spurred the brightest to disprove the Michelson-Morley result—but to no avail: based upon what has since been termed Newtonian physics, the finding stands solid as a rock. Eventually it was a young physicist, named Albert Einstein, who in the year 1905 broke the impasse with his so-called "theory of relativity" by discarding the Newtonian premises. Now, one might think that Einsteinian physics—at last—exonerates Galileo; but actually, it does nothing of the kind. What it implies, rather, is that physics *per se* is neutral on the issue. Given two objects in space, which of them "moves" depends upon a choice of reference frame, and it is a fundamental principle of Einsteinian physics that one reference frame is as legitimate as another.

Where, then, does this leave the famous—some would say infamous—trial: was it Galileo or was it the Church that erred? The crucial fact to be grasped is that this question cannot be resolved on the basis of physics: of physical science *per se*. To comprehend what actually stands at issue one needs first of all to distinguish categorically between the *physical* universe—the world as conceived by the physicist—and the *corporeal*: the *perceptible* world namely, which is evidently the one in which we find ourselves. The point is that these two ontological realms are not the same, and that the reduction of the corporeal to the physical—so far from being in any way justifiable on scientific grounds—constitutes in truth a scientistic fiction. I would argue, moreover, that it constitutes in fact the *foundational* scientistic fallacy: the one upon which all the rest are premised.

One sees thus in retrospect that Galileo's claim was an overreach on the part of science: to be precise, it constitutes in fact the very fallacy which in a fundamental way *defines* the modern era as such. And one might add that whereas, in the year 1616 the clerical advocates of geocentrism were for the most part simply "defending the status quo," Cardinal Bellarmine for his part recognized even in those days that the heliocentrist claim *is* an overreach, and argued the case with exemplary clarity. Yet it is doubtful that even the saintly Cardinal could have foreseen how deadly that overreach would eventually prove to be for mankind at large. Today one can see, in retrospect, that Galileo was in essence indeed the first authentically *modern* man. No wonder St. Malachy, in his famous prophesies, characterizes this period—which falls under the reign of Pope Paul V—by alluding to the birth of "a perverse race": how prophetic indeed! For it is now, four hundred years later, that the full implications of that fateful "birth"—its veritable "perversity"—are clearly and unmistakably coming to light.

Getting back to the Ptolemaic cosmography, I would point out that so far from exemplifying "primitive" science or "pagan superstition," that cosmography constitutes in fact a remnant of that "pre-Christian Christological knowledge" Malachi Martin had discovered in his paleographic inquiries. The reason, moreover, why this ancient teaching may strike us today as "primitive" or even absurd resides in the fact that we are constrained to perceive that cosmography through "modern" eyes: eyes which, in a fundamental sense, *no longer see.* So far as the Western world is concerned, Dante may indeed have been one of the last of our race who did have "eyes to see." Our present situation, thus, is comparable to that of a layman confronted with a paleographic specimen: where Malachi Martin perceives fragments of a Christological knowledge, he for his part sees simply a piece of rock with curious markings.

**You speak of the Ptolemaic cosmography with evident respect. Are you implying that it does indeed derive from that "pre-Christian Christological knowledge" to which Malachi Martin alludes, which constitutes as you say a "Christological cosmology"?**

I am implying precisely that. The pre-Christian Christological knowledge has given rise to what may broadly be termed *sacred* sciences. "Sacred" here means two things: first, that unlike our modern sciences, they derive from that Christological knowledge by way of a transmission, a kind of initiatory chain from master to disciple extending back into the mists of prehistory; and it also signifies that the ultimate objects of these sciences are none other than the *cosmic manifestations of Christ.*

Getting back to the Ptolemaic cosmography, beginning with the so-called seven planets: it needs first of all to be understood that these are not simply bodies in space as conceived by modern astronomers, but something to be *seen*: something, therefore, which in addition to quantitative determinants owns *qualities* as well. Let me emphasize that nothing void of qualities is actually visible or in any way *seeable*. What moreover distinguishes modern physical science categorically from the bona-fide sciences of antiquity is ultimately the fact that, strictly speaking, post-Galilean physics refers exclusively to *quantities*: *measurable* quantities to be precise. Yet even so—and notwithstanding the opinions of René Descartes and his followers—*qualities* likewise exist in the real world, and strange as it may sound to modern ears, are in a sense *more* real than the spatio-temporally grounded quantities of the physicist.

The *real* is ultimately *the seeable* in the widest and deepest sense of that term. It is moreover to be noted that whereas nothing void of qualities can actually be seen, the seeable does include quantities as well: integers first of all are obviously perceptible in both visual and auditory mode, as are their ratios, which in fact form the basis of musical harmony. The irony however is that the perceptible is categorically *imperceptible* to the physicist: what *he* perceives—or better said, *conceives*—are things defined in purely quantitative terms, entities therefore bereft of all qualities. It follows, based upon what I have said, that these "physical" entities *do not in truth exist*—a fact which, curiously enough, was clearly acknowledged by Werner Heisenberg (one of the founders of quantum theory) in reference to the so-called fundamental particles: they are something "midway between nonbeing and reality" as he put it. I will mention in passing that they actually belong to an ontological realm answering to what the Scholastics termed *potency* as distinguished from *act*.

The point I wish to make is that in excluding qualities *per se* from his purview by his very *modus operandi*, the physical scientist has in principle excluded the real itself. His situation is thus reminiscent of the "prisoners" alluded to in Plato's famous myth: men constrained to look at shadows projected upon the wall of a cave. To be precise: what the physicist *per se* perceives, so far from constituting the real, are but methodically elicited *effects* thereof—mere "shadows" as Plato has it—while the real itself, everything in fact that is *seeable*, has been excluded on *a priori* grounds. No wonder modern man is fundamentally confused; and no wonder too that the ancient sciences—to the extent that he is aware of them at all—strike him as childish and absurd. For those, on the other hand, still capable of grasping that the sky is blue, the case stands otherwise. If there be a science of the real, there must *ipso facto* be sciences that fit the pre-Galilean genre; and these sciences, moreover, must indeed be *Christological* for the simple reason that the cosmos is in fact a *theophany*, and thus *a manifestation*, ultimately, *of Christ*.

Let this much suffice to "situate" the Ptolemaic cosmography as a remnant of what I have termed generically the "sacred" sciences. We have evidently broached a field which, in its own way, is perforce "technical" and thus impenetrable "from the outside." To access that subject—not in fantasy but in truth—it is moreover necessary, first of all, to free oneself from a whole gamut of contemporary misconceptions: to unlearn what has been bred into us for centuries—ever since the fateful year 1616 if you will! Uninformed speculation—let alone the opinions of modern-day pundits—cannot but lead us astray. What I do want however to convey on the subject are three fundamental facts: i.e., that there *are* such ancient sciences, that they are utterly different from our own, and that they do indeed derive from that "pre-Christian Christological knowledge" to which Malachi Martin alludes.

**You spoke earlier of an urgent need for a "Christological cosmology," and now you maintain that the "sciences" expressive of that cosmology are in their own way "technical" and "impenetrable from the outside." But how can such a cosmology benefit society or the Church? How can sciences which hardly anyone understands impact an entire culture?**

In the first place let me point out that we have a very pertinent example of that seemingly impossible scenario in the case of contemporary physics, a science which indeed "hardly anyone understands," but which has nonetheless exerted a decisive impact upon our entire culture. What presently concerns us is the ideological as distinguished from the technological impact of physical science upon our civilization: the worldview it has imposed upon one and all, including individuals who could not get past freshman calculus. To be affected ideologically by physical

41

science it is by no means necessary to penetrate the esoteric world of quantum theory.

The case is similar when it comes to the ancient sciences, but with one highly notable difference: the worldview to which these sciences give rise is not adventitious, but actually founded upon the verities these sciences discern. Though "impenetrable from the outside," these truths can in a way be intuited by any receptive man, woman or child—but not in their "technical" explication. The reason for this accessibility resides in the fact that the ancient sciences, no matter how "esoteric," deal yet with what is in a sense *perceptible*. And in this respect they differ categorically from our contemporary physical sciences, which have to do with aggregates of so-called "particles" that most assuredly are not *visible* in any sense whatsoever. Not only, therefore, are these sciences "impenetrable from the outside," but they do not *de jure* give rise to a "worldview" at all: there simply is no way one can "view" a proton or electron, entities which must consequently remain incomprehensible to anyone lacking the mathematical tools in terms of which they are defined. As objects constituent of a worldview they are consequently fraudulent: mere idols of the mind as the ancients might say. It is indeed ironic that in the name of the most accurate science the world has ever known, civilization has fallen prey to a spurious myth.

Having stated that we stand today in urgent need of the traditional sciences, let me elucidate what this means. It obviously does *not* mean that everyone needs to be instructed in one or more of these sciences! What is called for on the part of the general public is simply an awareness of the fact that these sciences exist: that there are indeed "more things in heaven and earth, Horatio" than are dreamt of in our present-day "philosophy." We need to recover the realization—*de jure* normal and normative for mankind—that the cosmos and all that exists therein harbors a supernatural core: it is this truth, this recognition of "Christ at the Center of all things," that saints and mystics, in particular, seize upon and occasionally attest by the miracles they perform. If the cosmos were in truth the material entity we of the present age take it to be, religion would be reduced inexorably to the status of a fantasy, a mere "psychotherapy" at best. And is this not, after all, the view that nowadays obtrudes itself—even, it would appear, within the precincts of the Church? We denizens of the brave new world have all but lost the sense of the supernatural, the sense of "mystery" which constitutes the very oxygen of true religion.

You asked how sciences which hardly anyone understands can impact an entire culture, and we have cited two examples, which in a sense are polar opposites.

**Can you tell us how you yourself became acquainted with what you term the sacred sciences, and have arrived at your conclusions in their regard?**

That is quite a long story. Suffice it to say that my philosophical studies—especially in the fields of Platonism and Neoplatonism—have early on put me on the spoor of these "lost" sciences, following which I traveled to various parts of the world where vestiges of such ancient traditions are still to be found. It was thus finally "by word of mouth" that I learned a few things about these matters—but I should add: not until my mind had been thoroughly purged of our contemporary preconceptions. Reading Plato may have been a necessary preparation, but did not suffice: a radical change of environment, a certain "living touch" if you will, was also needed. What is hardest, I would say, is to "unlearn."

One thing, however, I did have going for me from the start, and that is respect, a sense of *reverence*. Instinctively, as it were, I approached the *vera philosophia* and the sciences based thereon "with folded hands." It was in fact the conspicuous absence of that sensibility vis-à-vis "the sacred" among faculty and students alike that drove me out of the philosophy department at Cornell. There is always of course a danger that one might approach the wrong thing "with folded hands"; and yet I believe that where the motive is right, the good angel will eventually put us back upon the "straight and narrow" path of truth.

Once, long ago, I had a book inscribed by a visiting monk from a far-away land: *"There is nothing holier than truth"* the inscription reads. Little did I know then how literally true this is: for I had not yet learned that Truth is Christ Himself.

# Part III
## How to Survive as a Catholic in an Anti-Catholic World

**I would like now to touch upon an article you wrote for the *Homiletic & Pastoral Review*, entitled "The Demon of Distraction." One could say that this article discusses the problem of the modern world. Do you think this problem is worse now than when you wrote the article?**

I am glad you raised this question. So far, we have been discussing issues pertaining to the theoretical order; let us shift now to the realm of praxis, of "real life" if you will. The article you cite deals with "*distraction*" as a fundamental problem universal to mankind, which has however become progressively exacerbated in the modern world. Yet "distractedness" is rarely recognized as an anomaly, nor commented upon from a spiritual point of vantage. I don't recall ever hearing the subject mentioned in a sermon or discussed in a pastoral setting; and yet distraction *per se* is deadly to the spiritual life, and reaching epidemic proportions as we speak.

It is hardly needful to define the word: distraction is evidently a scattering of the mind—the very opposite of *concentration*, which is to set the mind upon one thing, even as a marksman fixes his gaze upon the center of a target. It should moreover be obvious that success in whatever venture depends largely upon our ability to concentrate, and thus to perceive what is essential— the big picture—as opposed to a scattering of impressions. Strictly speaking, to see a "picture" at all—even in the case of ordinary sense perception—requires concentration of a kind. It is the power or act which transforms a scattered multitude into a recognizable object by revealing its center, its "point"; and let me note in passing that no neurophysiologist has yet been able to explain—even remotely—how this feat is accomplished. In fact, the neuroscientist cannot comprehend it at all: the force or power in question escapes his net. For it pertains in truth to what the Scholastics termed *intellect*: a faculty that literally "is not of this world."

We are beginning to see that concentration—and thus also distraction by default—has indeed a *spiritual* significance. Nor need we be surprised: did not Christ call upon us repeatedly to *concentrate*, most explicitly perhaps when He declared: "*Let your eye be single*." There is a profound metaphysical significance in this logion which has been almost universally missed. Among the three so-called transcendentals conceived as "names of God"—the True, the Good, and the One—it is "the One" that in a certain sense holds primacy: for it alone designates God in His ultimate Ground, His unfathomable Depth. The pertinent point is that *all oneness*—from that of the smallest insect to the universe at large—derives from the One, and in a way "presentifies" that Oneness. Or to put it another way: if our mental eye were truly "*single*"—if we were truly "*pure in heart*"—what we would behold in the "oneness" of all created beings is indeed the presence of God. The problem, however, is that we are endowed—on account of Original Sin—with a *centrifugal* tendency which needs to be overcome: "*He that gathereth not with me scattereth*" says the Lord—and it hardly needs pointing out that distraction is precisely a "scattering."

It is becoming apparent that *distraction*—somewhat like *liberalism*—is in effect a "sin" even though it has no official status as such, and no one bothers to say much about it. The purpose, thus, of my article in the *Homiletic & Pastoral Review*, was to alert the clergy, in particular, to the fact that there is a major problem here which needs to be addressed; and I am happy to note that the paper did in fact set off a flurry of debate and articles regarding this issue. But of course the problem remains, and in fact looms larger with every passing year. I think you may well be right, Bernard, in referring to it as "*the* problem of the modern world": chronic distractedness, after all, is literally a *disintegration* of the person in the very component which renders us human—i.e., the *mind*—and it is the modern world that exacerbates this fatal condition to a hitherto unimaginable degree.

In 1981, when I published my article, that onslaught against our humanity was yet, comparatively speaking, in its infancy, the dominant source of distraction at the time being television. The problem was of course particularly acute and tragic in the case of children and adolescents, who should be using these formative years to develop their mental and physical capabilities instead of sitting in front of a TV screen, I forget how many hours per week, absorbing a bewildering medley of stimuli, the informational content of which is for the most part useless. Leaving aside the fact that television was at the time the most powerful instrument of indoctrination and mass hypnosis the world had ever seen, I chose to consider it simply as a source of distraction.

But to answer the rest of your question: the problem has indeed worsened dramatically in the intervening decades. Entirely new technologies have been developed, flooding the market with portable devices which in effect bring that electronic "demon of distraction" into just about every segment of our life. Whether we are eating a meal or waiting for a bus, the "demon" is right there, ready to flood our consciousness with an endless barrage of visual and auditory stimuli which might broadly be characterized as "noise." Leaving aside all other considerations, I would like to repeat that the effect of such an overstimulation upon our *spiritual* life cannot but be harmful in the extreme. Let me be clear: I do not deny for a moment that there are benefits to be derived from this astounding technology—that one can now, on an i-phone, avail oneself, let us say, of treatises housed in the Vatican library. My point, rather, is that there is a temptation to overindulge, to open our mind to an excess of stimuli which we cannot sift and assimilate, and that in fact this process, leading literally to "disintegration," has a tendency to feed upon itself, to worsen exponentially. And let us be clear: if the perception of unity leads ultimately to God, as I have tried to suggest, that centrifugal drift takes us, quite clearly, in the opposite direction. It is therefore dangerously inimical to the Christian life: literally a "scattering" as opposed to a "gathering with Christ."

**There is a trend for more and more information-gathering to be conducted on the internet rather than from books. Do you think that this trend has its negative aspects, as the depth of most information on the internet is shallower than in books?**

You have raised a major issue. The internet has become a prime factor in contemporary civilization: an influence of incomparable magnitude upon the population at large; it therefore

46

behooves us to consider the impact of this technological prodigy not only from a commercial and utilitarian point of view, but also—and above all—with reference to our intellectual and spiritual formation. While I am by no means an authority on this topic (since I myself don't use the internet), I do surmise that the depth of "most information" carried in that medium "is shallower than in books"—which is hardly surprising, given that everyone is free to post just about anything. It is thus left to the discretion of the viewer to select what he views: to choose whether it be some piece of tripe, or a Patristic commentary, let us say, on the Psalms. And in this immeasurable leeway resides perhaps the prime danger posed by the internet: one fears that without proper education and guidance it may be the former category that will generally take precedence.

Yet even for the discerning reader who knows how to avoid what is worthless, misleading or offensive, there remains yet the danger posed by the sheer quantity of good and highly worthwhile offerings—which is to say that, here again, we are confronted by "the demon of distraction." The great temptation is to scatter the mind by ingesting countless bits of sundry information from here and there, which in the end—like Shakespeare's "tale told by an idiot"—"signifies nothing." I think we have all come across nominally educated people whose mind has become a jumble of unassimilated snippets of heaven knows what, which they will articulate at the least provocation, thereby bringing to an abrupt close what could otherwise have been an intelligent conversation.

One last point I would make: in the final count, nothing can replace a good book. I mean one that is not only of quality in its content, but well-crafted to boot—leather-bound perhaps—which even as a tangible object constitutes a work of art. Such a book brings pleasure and a certain ennoblement even when one holds it in one's hands; it speaks to one, just as other works of art do. The question will of course be raised: what on earth do these outer trappings have to do with the book's worth as an intellectual document? Well, the fact is they do—even perhaps as the suit a professor wears when giving a lecture has also its significance. If a book has a content, it has an outer face as well; and as is the case in all of God's creation, so also in artifacts, the inner and the outer—content and container if you will—should be compatible, should be well matched. My claim—which by contemporary standards is as meaningless as it is unprovable—is that in the case of electronic text rendered visible on a computer screen, that organismal harmony has been categorically impaired, with the result that the reader of internet text never quite gets out of what may be termed the artificial environment. That at least is my contention, which I put out knowing full well that "the man of today" will not have a ghost of an idea what in the world I am talking about.

**You have taught at American universities for many years. Are there dangers to the faith of Catholic students who attend today's universities?**

To begin with, universities have been a threat to the Catholic faith ever since the Enlightenment. Take the Europe in which I was born: the true undiluted Catholic faith was to be found, generally speaking, in segments of the population far removed culturally from the so-called centers of higher education. Meanwhile the problem has worsened progressively, in Europe no less than in America, and today our universities threaten not only the faith, but one might almost say, the very sanity of our youth. Professors tend—almost without exception—to be of a radically liberal bent and bias, even if perchance they admit to being Christians. To give but one example: virtually every member of the academic community, in whatever faculty, believes nowadays in so-called "religious liberty"—the notion that we have the unmitigated right of "choosing" our religious tenets—a claim which theologically makes little sense. Only God could bestow upon us that right, and quite obviously He has done nothing of the kind. On the contrary: He has *revealed* religious truths and made it clear that we are henceforth obligated to abide by the commandments they entail. We are "free" of course to do as we will: but we do so at our own risk, in peril of our soul. Yet, when it comes to the aficionados of "liberty"—whether they profess to be Christians or not—this deadly warning falls invariably upon deaf ears.

The acute danger to the faith of Catholic students to which you allude is magnified by the fact that this liberal mentality is

48

highly contagious: that it tends to impose itself by contact so to speak, by mere proximity. What renders this pervasive influence well-nigh irresistible, moreover, is the fact that it enjoys, as I have said, the imprimatur of the faculty at large: that this entire gamut of liberal tenets is in fact sanctioned and promoted by authority figures of the highest standing in our secular world. Typically, the ideas in question—the notion, for instance, that mankind has gradually emancipated itself from superstitious and barbarous beliefs through the advance of science—are treated as discoveries arrived at by way of that very advance or "evolution" of mankind: a circular and almost totally inverted notion, which nonetheless enjoys in the academic world the status of an indubitable truth. Now, it is obviously too much to expect from a student that he can, on his own cognizance, stand up to these seductive claims, which today enjoy the endorsement of virtually the entire so-called "educated" world. Humanly speaking, the case is hopeless—which is to say that what is actually called for to preserve the faith of a Catholic student is the intervention of a *supernatural* factor, be it through an act of devotion, an inspiration from his guardian angel, or by whatever spiritual means. What counts is the grace of God: on a purely "human" level the battle can hardly even begin, much less can it be won.

**The situation of modern universities presents a dilemma for Catholic families. On one hand, we need good Catholic doctors, lawyers, scientists, etc. At the same time, the way modern universities are set up can endanger the faith of Catholic students. What are some ways of dealing with the dilemma?**

It is essential, above all, to provide the student-to-be with the best possible foundation before he or she ever sets foot on a university campus. Even as one vaccinates people before letting them enter a disease-infested region, it is imperative to endow the prospective student with the requisite "antibodies" to safeguard against infection. The single most important element, to be sure, is the spiritual formation: a grounding not only in sound Christian doctrine, but in the spiritual life, by which I mean the well-nigh "natural" practice of Catholic devotions, such as kneeling before an icon or praying at the foot of an altar, and most especially, the daily recitation of the Rosary. I realize that these practices have been neglected and to a large extent abandoned in the Novus Ordo culture, which is a prime reason to seek out a traditional Catholic church as well as the guidance of a traditional priest. It is needless to add that the reading of solid spiritual books—like the *Confessions of St. Augustine* or the biography of a saint, from the Fathers to St. Catherine of Siena, for instance, or St. Padre Pio in our day—has a profound effect on our spiritual and indeed intellectual formation.

In addition, it is expedient to introduce the university aspirant during his or her high school years to some of the main issues at stake in the current assault against Catholic tradition, beginning perhaps with the subject of "evolution." What commends this topic as a suitable starting point is first of all the fact that the Darwinist thesis proves to be basic to the contemporary "science-based" Weltanschauung which has imposed itself upon virtually every facet of contemporary civilization, including the post-Conciliar Church. Today that science-fiction fantasy affects just about every facet of our outlook and turns everything it touches upside-down. In addition, Darwinism as a topic to be scrutinized offers the advantage that its refutation at the hands of contemporary scientific dissenters can in the main be understood by the non-specialist, and that there exists today a very readable literature which exposes the fraud as clearly as one could wish.

Turning to the explicitly ideological side of the modernist spectrum, we face a syndrome of beliefs and values that might in truth be subsumed under the caption of Liberalism—and I would recall that Liberalism is indeed "a sin," given that, in just about every one of its facets it cuts against the Christian norm. This too, therefore, is a domain in which the prospective university student needs to establish some points of reference; and here as well it is expedient to avail oneself of a suitable literature. Certainly, there are books that can serve this purpose, and I might mention that there are also periodical publications, such as *Catholic Family News* or *Latin Mass Magazine*, that provide useful insight. And last but not least, there is the medium of informed conversation— above all with a traditional priest or some wise elder—which may be the single most effective means of all to prepare a young person for the "battle" he is to face.

Once arrived on campus, one of the first things to be attended to is to ascertain which courses *not* to take. A prime example would be any course which has the word "psychology" in its title: avoid it, I say, like the plague. So too stay clear of the Philosophy Department (unless perchance you happen to be at Cambridge University!). Concentrate, according to your interests, on solid courses in science, engineering, pre-medicine or even jurisprudence, if you are so inclined. So-called "liberal arts" subjects are to be carefully scrutinized; if it be literature, for instance, see whether it focuses upon Milton say, or Shakespeare, or on the likes of Marcel Proust; and in any case, be on your guard: chances are good your professor of literature will be a raving liberal. There will also, of course, be raving liberals among your fellow students; and if you can find a like-minded friend, you are very fortunate indeed. In any case, select your company, and also learn to spend time fruitfully by yourself: it seems that a bit of loneliness proves to be a *sine qua non* these days for rising above the prevailing mediocrity.

**Why do you single out psychology as a subject to be "avoided like the plague"?**

To be specific, let us consider the doctrines of Sigmund Freud and Carl Jung, the two founders, if you will, of modern psychology. In the first place, I would say that neither of their theories actually qualifies as "science"—so long of course as one uses that term in its accepted connotation. To be sure, there are "observations" in the thousands, "data" if you will: the point, however, is that data alone do not suffice. Everything hinges upon the *modus operandi* by which one passes from such raw empirical facts to the conclusions based thereon: there must be an underlying logic which guarantees the legitimacy of that deduction and distinguishes its inference from a mere opinion. And this, I say, is the missing element in both Freudian and Jungian psychology: in the final count these sweeping psychological conclusions—so dear to millions!—are based upon nothing more substantial than the ideological bias of their respective proponent. It is interesting, moreover, that Jung—a fallen-away disciple of Freud—admits as

51

much in reference to his former mentor: after debunking just about every facet of the Freudian teaching—while *à la* Freud, no less, ascribing these to various idiosyncrasies of the master himself— he goes so far as to offer an observation which cuts to the core: "Today the voice of one crying in the wilderness," he writes, "must necessarily strike a scientific tone if the ear of the multitude is to be reached...": how very true indeed! What of course Jung does *not* say is that this revelation applies to his own doctrine as well.

As I have pointed out repeatedly, contemporary science never stands alone, but is accompanied invariably by ideological premises and ideology-based extrapolations masquerading in scientific garb. What however is special in the case of contemporary psychology at large is the fact that such extrapolations tend to be all: that there *is no* hard currency accompanying the counterfeit. It should moreover be pointed out that much the same can be said regarding the so-called social sciences: the tons of data, for the most part statistical, are real enough; what seems to be lacking in general, on the other hand, is a rigorous *modus operandi* that could justify the conclusions supposedly based thereon. The reason, however, why I have singled out psychology is that among all contemporary pseudo-sciences—of which there are many—psychology is by far the most lethal due to the fact that it clearly and unabashedly infringes upon the domain of *the sacred* which rightfully pertains to the sphere of religion. What the likes of Freud and Jung have to offer a spiritually starved and craving public *is* in fact a religion of sorts: an *Ersatz-* or *pseudo-religion*, to be precise.

### Is it accurate to put Freud and Jung in the same category, since Jung, unlike Freud, was a believer in religion?

Freud and Jung both belong to the category of "highly dangerous" modern-day gurus at large who in the name of "science" have foisted upon an unsuspecting public ideas and practices of the most pernicious kind. But whereas Sigmund Freud debunks religion as a psychological aberration, Carl Jung—again "striking a scientific tone"—claims to have discovered its rationale in the collective unconscious, thereby depriving religion *per se* of its revelatory basis. It is hard to say which of these deceptions has caused the greater devastation and perdition of souls.

Freud no less than his apostate disciple, each in his own way, has supplied a substitute for authentic religion: an Ersatz as I have said. Freud for his part—in keeping with his fixation upon "repressed sexuality"—has in effect replaced religion by a program of unabashed erotic indulgence offered as the universal panacea for most of what ails us, and I would add that one need hardly be surprised that prospective disciples from all parts of the western world have flocked to the Viennese sage in droves, and that Hollywood has sponsored a whole genre of films celebrating his salvific wisdom.

The Jungian recipe for the attainment of beatitude, on the other hand, is considerably more refined, and has generally attracted the better educated strata of society, including not a few Catholic intellectuals: a well known Dominican, for example, has gone so far as to refer to the Swiss psychiatrist as "a priest without a surplice"! Jung shares in fact with Teilhard de Chardin the dubious distinction of having promulgated a "scientific" version of Christianity that dispenses supposedly from "blind belief" and submission to an institutionalized priesthood. Yet that is about the only thing the two modern-day prophets have in common: in every other respect Jung and Teilhard are virtually polar opposites, and their respective versions of a "scientific" Christianity could not be more antithetical. It seems that Jung is there to "catch" the more introspective and potentially "mystical" among believers and unbelievers alike.

**Getting back to what could be done to protect the faith of Catholic students attending these universities: do you think that one solution might be to establish good Catholic residences which would act to sustain their faith?**

I think "good Catholic residences" could certainly help to protect the faith of students and prevent them from straying into harmful ways. As Christians, we know what strength is to be derived from an authentic communion of the faithful; one needs but to recall the words of our Lord: *"Where two or three are gathered in my name, there am I in their midst."*

The problem, however, is that we no longer live in an age

when pagans were wont to exclaim: "Look how these Christians love each other!" The world at large has grown cold, and we Catholics have cooled down as well. As a rule, authentic love—as distinguished from its vocal declaration—is confined more or less to the circle of one's immediate family.

What is more, communal life today is fraught with peril. Besides the perennial temptations, there is the ongoing plague of homosexuality which appears to be assuming epidemic proportions in western society. All things considered, it may be advisable for a student to limit his or her closer social contacts to a few chosen companions instead of running the risk of contamination through membership in a community. In addition, it seems that just about every form of communal life these days entails some kind of reduction to a status quo—a certain collective mediocrity one might almost say—which a person with higher aspirations might want to avoid. There are of course different ways and aptitudes, and what is best for one person may not be suitable for another.

Yet notwithstanding these reservations, I think that, *given the right circumstances*, Catholic residences could indeed be beneficial, as I have said; one needs however to realize that these conditions are not easily met. First of all, to be authentically Catholic, a residence of this kind would have to be somehow associated with a church or chapel, a site of worship; but alas, the official Church itself, as we know, has been modernized! It is obviously futile therefore to look to the Novus Ordo churchmen for protection against the onslaughts of modernity: it is they who need to be, more often than not, set straight in that regard. Conceivably the project could enlist the patronage of a traditional priestly association, be it the Fraternity of St. Peter or the Society of St. Pius X; however, realistically speaking, this entails that the project could be realized only at a few select institutions, which in itself may pose a variety of problems.

But perhaps you are referring to something of a more modest kind: say a group of traditionally-minded Catholic students—a handful perhaps—banding together in a shared residence to lend each other support; and that, it seems to me—though still not unproblematic—is something well within the range of possibility, which yet might be of significant benefit. I know from my own life experience that there were times when I would have given much for the company of just a single kindred soul!

What actually stands at issue, as I see it, is a kind of Catholic comradeship, something intrinsically of immense significance. I have read that even the hermits at Mount Athos leave their solitary abode periodically to meet with comrades, presumably to share their thoughts and aspirations. It seems that such a fraternal exchange—such a sharing of insight and values—constitutes in principle an integral part of the Christian life, be it of hermits or of ordinary people trying to follow Christ in their particular calling.

I would however point out that such communion with fellow Christians can be fostered and achieved in various ways. Besides the establishment of Catholic residences, it can evidently be realized through association, when possible, with an authentic Catholic parish, which constitutes perhaps the most obvious and natural option. Periodic visits to one's home base—in imitation of those hermits!—may also be helpful; and even a single true friend—more than a small handful one may scarcely hope for in this life!—can make a world of difference. If all of us, moreover, have need for some form of companionship with those who share our holy Catholic faith, how great must be that necessity in the case of young people herded into the precincts of a modern-day university like lambs led to the slaughter!

**Would you say that Christian university students must adopt the traditional Catholic mindset of being in the world, but not of the world? Does the university student of today have to be like a mouse who takes the cheese (a university degree), but does not get caught?**

I believe the "traditional Catholic mindset" to which you refer has indeed become a *sine qua non* necessity for university students bent upon keeping their faith. As I indicated earlier, the pressure upon Christian believers within the university environment to embrace the credo and ideals of the reigning liberal majority is simply overwhelming, all the more since the mentality in question presents itself as tolerant in regard to just about all forms of belief.

One needs indeed to be "wise as a serpent" not to be taken in, not to succumb to the ruling mentality which knows very well how to proselytize. Whether it be on the strength of his own perceptions or simply by the grace of God, the Catholic student needs to understand that he finds himself in an ambience which—despite claims of universal tolerance—is in fact uncompromisingly hostile to Christianity.

What presently renders this discernment all the more difficult is the fact that for the past fifty years the "institutional Church" has been teaching the very opposite. Ever since the inebriating days of the Council, as we know, *aggiornamento* has become the law of the land. It is a lot to ask, therefore, of a present-day Catholic—a student no less—to stand up not only to the intellectual elite of our civilization, but to the guidelines issued by Catholic churchmen of even the highest rank. Yet the miracle does happen, and far more often in fact than one might think: truly, faith can "move mountains"!

To be "in the world, but not of the world" is of course an immemorial precept of the Church going back to the teaching of Christ, which calls upon every Christian, wherever he may be, to contend against the proclivity to conform to the world, to make its values and its ways his own—which is after all the reason why the Church here below is designated by the epithet "militant." My contention, however, is that there are times and places in which this universal precept acquires an exceptional urgency, and that the contemporary university is indeed a case in point.

Certainly, I concur with your example of the mouse that takes the cheese without getting caught in the trap. It reminds me in fact of the epithet *"paramahamsa,"* one of the highest titles bestowed in India upon a man of God. Now the word *"hamsa"* means *swan*: what is it, then, about a swan that carries over to sages of the highest rank? The answer derives from the belief that when presented with a mixture of milk and water, a swan is able to separate the two and partake of the milk alone (a feat it accomplishes, we are told, by secreting an acid which curdles the milk). So too the *paramahamsa*—literally the great or "supreme" swan—is able to take from the waters of this world what is in it of God, and reject the rest.

56

**In conclusion, do you think that the message that Malachi Martin worked so tirelessly to promote when he was alive is still relevant today?**

In light of events presently unfolding within the Catholic Church as well as in civil society, I have no doubt that Malachi Martin's message is in fact more visibly relevant today than it was when he first startled a generally incredulous public with his well-nigh apocalyptic depiction of major trends. It is becoming clearer with each passing year that Malachi Martin was not only a great historian, but something of a prophet as well. Nor need one be surprised: for it happens that whosoever penetrates into the inner workings of history beyond a certain depth is sure also to garner a glimpse of the future. Add to this the fact that Malachi Martin, as a master exorcist, was privy to insights relating to the demonic realm—which, as we should all understand, is hyperactive these days—and one begins to see how he was able to discern what for most of us is hidden as if by an impenetrable veil.

It appears that, at its deepest level, Malachi Martin's understanding of the world and its history was in fact *Christological*. And again, this should not surprise us: as Christians we know that Christ, being God Himself, resides at the very Center of all things, visible and invisible, and that whatsoever transpires in the universe falls under His jurisdiction. The Kingship of Christ, thus, refers not only to human society, but to the cosmos at large; for "in Him resides all the fullness of the Godhead *bodily* (*somatikos*)" as St. Paul apprises us. At this depth, the picture has radically changed: in place of a mere assembly of creatures, everything is now focused upon Christ. At the same time, however a second Figure comes likewise into view: for where here below there is Light, there is also perforce an ambient Darkness. Or to put it another way: where there is a Victor, there must likewise be an Adversary. In the final count, Lucifer is not an accident—not merely something or someone gone awry—but a *sine qua non* in the dynamics of our universe. From the outset the Adversary is there, foreseen and demanded in the inscrutable Plan of God. In the words of Goethe's Mephisto to Faust: "I am a part of that Force which ever seeks evil and is ever productive of good." What confronts us here and now—in a manner ultimately beyond human conception—is a combat *sui generis* between two Opponents personifying Light and Darkness respectively: i.e., *Christ* and Antichrist. Everywhere in the universe, seen and unseen, this Warfare rages; and herein undoubtedly is to be found the ultimate dynamic of world history.

The question now obtrudes: where does this leave man? How do *we* fit into the picture? And in the sharpest conceivable contrast to the humanist credo—our present-day "religion of man"—it happens that we are left with *only one* truly free choice: we can and indeed *must* choose with which of the two "Forces" we wish to align ourselves: in which of the "two cities" we shall henceforth abide, to put it in St. Augustine's metaphor. And let me emphasize that, in the final count, this is actually the only choice we can *freely* make, the one and only authentically free act of which we are capable: for the rest, our vaunted claims of "freedom" and "self-sufficiency" are based on humanist hubris and nothing more.

But let us note: paltry as it may seem to the children of this world, this God-given freedom to choose between Light and Darkness—between Christ and Antichrist—is the greatest treasure we possess, the highest *conceivable* Gift we can ever receive: for it—and it alone!—can open for us the Path to Salvation, to the Highest Good which is Life Eternal, what some theologians refer to even as a *deificatio*.

It is hardly needful to say that Malachi Martin understood all this in depth: more profoundly, I surmise, than most of us can conceive. To be sure, he disposed over a vast array of historical, political and even economic facts; but unlike our pundits, he perceived all this, as I have said, from a *Christological* point of view. The closer his friends came to know this priest, the more clearly they realized that his life was wholly dedicated to Christ, the Incarnate God. In the course of my first conversation with Malachi Martin, after I had spoken to him of my spiritual endeavors and aspirations, he said to me quite simply: "Remember: Christ is very powerful." I must admit that I was somewhat disappointed by this response: it seemed to me at the time almost trite. *Of course*, Christ is "very powerful"! Yes; but did I understand what this actually means? To discover what Malachi Martin was in fact telling me, one requires a capacity to divine the dimension of depth: the very depth at which the combat between Christ and Antichrist is actually waged. What does it mean, then, to say that "Christ is very powerful"? It means, quite simply, that *He always wins*.

This, I like to think, may well be the central message Malachi Martin has bequeathed to posterity in his capacity as a priest and spiritual director: to enlighten our understanding, to guide and strengthen us in our tribulations, and to bestow upon us a joy the world can never take away. It is no wonder that those who knew Fr. Martin best look upon him as a saint.

**At the core of Malachi Martin's message is the idea that there is being waged a cosmic battle between those forces who are for Christ and those forces who are against Christ. Do you actually mean to say that we cannot stay neutral in this battle?**

I am not sure neutrality is in truth an option even in the short term: in the long run, in any case, it most assuredly is not. We are on earth for no other reason than to opt for life eternal in God: to avail ourselves, in other words, of this truly infinite gift proffered by Christ, which unlike lesser conferrals requires an act of free will on our part for its reception. Eternal beatitude, it seems, is the one thing God cannot "thrust upon us": the one objective He seemingly cannot accomplish simply "by Himself." We too have a part to play in this consummation; our assent and cooperation are needed for the reception of the gift, and these we are free to bestow or to withhold: we are born, in the final count, for no other purpose than to make this infinitely fateful choice. Neutrality is not in truth an option, for in its own way neutrality itself constitutes a choice: the wrong choice namely: *"He who is not with me is against me,"* Christ declares.

Actually, we are called to do more than simply "opt for Christ": we are obliged to back this decision with action when the occasion demands. To cry *"Lord, Lord"* is not enough: we need also *"to do the will of my Father."* As members of what has been most aptly termed the "Church Militant," we need in fact to do so with fortitude and zeal; as the Angel declared to the Laodiceans: *"So then because thou art lukewarm, and neither cold nor hot, I will spew thee out of my mouth."* One recalls perhaps the infernal abode to which Dante assigns these "Laodicean" souls, with the stinging comment: "I had not thought death had undone so many."

It is essential that we grasp Malachi Martin's message in full: the truth is that we find ourselves neither in a good nor in an evil world, but literally in midst of a battlefield. The notion of a friendly and "peaceful" planet—a safe and happy place where warfare shall be no more—is but a humanist pipedream: an illusion promoted, in the final count, by the Antichrist, who has been striving from the outset to turn men's minds from Heaven to this earthly domain: from God's dispensation to his own counterfeit. This is a crucial point on which modern-day Catholics tend to be thoroughly misled: notwithstanding what we have been taught from pulpits over the past fifty years, the world is *not* in fact a children's playground. The warfare is real, and the enemy formidable in the extreme: "*For we wrestle not against flesh and blood, but against principalities, against powers, against the rulers of the darkness of this world, against spiritual wickedness in high places.*" The time is long overdue to engrave these words upon our hearts and minds.

There is a corollary to this Pauline logion which should likewise be thus enshrined: man is not in truth half as mighty and self-sufficient as our modern-day pundits have taught us to believe. In fact, taken by himself—with all his vaunted capacities and so-called "human dignity"—he is no match for even the shabbiest of the demons surrounding us on all sides. The only way a human being can be victorious in this titanic contest is in fact to ally himself with the Son of God; as Malachi Martin affirmed to me on that memorable day: "*Remember: Christ is very powerful.*"